THE THERAPIST'S TOOLKIT

QUESTIONNAIRES, WORKSHEETS, AND INFORMATION SHEETS TO ASSESS AND IMPROVE CLIENT PROBLEMS

CLYDE M. FELDMAN, Ph.D.

A Clyde Feldman, Ph.D. Publication

THE THERAPIST'S TOOLKIT

QUESTIONNAIRES, WORKSHEETS, AND INFORMATION SHEETS TO ASSESS AND IMPROVE CLIENT PROBLEMS

Copyright © 2013 Clyde M. Feldman, Ph.D.

All rights reserved.

Printed in the United States of America

All rights reserved. No part of this book may be reproduced or transmitted in any form or by any means, electronic or mechanical, including photocopying, recording, or by any information storage and retrieval system, without permission in writing from the publisher.

*****

Formatting By Debora Lewis
www.arenapublishing.org

ISBN-13: 978-1490453699
ISBN-10: 1490453695

THE THERAPIST'S TOOLKIT

QUESTIONNAIRES, WORKSHEETS, AND INFORMATION SHEETS TO ASSESS AND IMPROVE CLIENT PROBLEMS

SEVENTY QUESTIONNAIRES, WORKSHEETS, AND INFORMATION SHEETS DESIGNED TO IDENTIFY, ASSESS, AND IMPROVE CLIENT PROBLEMS IN THE AREAS OF: COMMUNICATION, CONFLICT, STRESS, ANGER, DOMESTIC VIOLENCE, ANXIETY, DEPRESSION, SUBSTANCE ABUSE, SEX ADDICTION, ADULT A.D.D., INTIMACY, JEALOUSY, ADULT ATTACHMENT, PERSONALITY DISORDERS, AND MORE.

CLYDE M. FELDMAN, Ph.D.

LICENSED MARRIAGE AND FAMILY THERAPIST
LICENSED PROFESSIONAL COUNSELOR
CERTIFIED NLP MASTER PRACTITIONER

TUCSON, AZ
(520) 326-6060
E-MAIL: CMFELDMAN@AOL.COM
WEB: COUNSELINGTOOLSTHATWORK.COM

PREFACE

The seventy questionnaires, worksheets, and information sheets included here are designed for counselors and therapists to use with their individual, couples, and group clients in order to facilitate and enhance the counseling process. The tools are self-help oriented and allow clients to be more involved in the process of identifying, exploring, and improving a wide range of problems.

The twenty worksheets are designed to guide clients through a set of skill-building steps for improving a particular problem.

The twenty-five information sheets are designed to provide clients with detailed information about a problem which has been condensed and "translated" so it's easy to understand and apply to their situation.

The twenty-five assessment instruments (i.e., questionnaires, checklists, inventories, and tests), are designed to provide detailed information about the signs and symptoms of a possible problem and it's degree of severity. However, completing the assessment instrument alone should not be the sole basis for making a clinical diagnosis. Your knowledge of the client's background, circumstances, history, and additional clinical problems are key in forming a complete picture of the problem. There are several reasons for this. They are:

1. Many problems addressed in counseling and therapy don't have a formal "clinical" definition that is agreed upon. Therefore, different definitions of the problem by researchers, practitioners, or "experts" might be used in different assessment instruments (e.g., stress, intimacy, jealousy, conflict, domestic violence, sex addiction, etc.).

2. Some problems do have a formal "clinical" definition based upon the Diagnostic and Statistical Manual (DSM), but developers of assessment instruments have expanded on that or modified that in developing their assessment instrument (e.g., substance abuse, A.D.D., etc.).

3. Even for problems that do have a formal "clinical" definition, the definitions often specify only whether one or more symptoms or characteristics is present or not present (e.g., loss of interest, racing mind). The definitions do not specify the degree of severity. Many assessment instruments, however, determine how severe the problem is without clear guidance from a "clinical" definition (e.g., depression, anxiety, bi-polar, etc.).

4. When individuals are answering questions by self-report, each person is answering subjectively and interpreting the questions differently for themselves, so their score may be quite different than another person's score who has a very similar problem or a very similar set of symptoms.

5. High scores on many assessment instruments may result from having symptoms or characteristics of a different problem or condition that has related or overlapping symptoms. For example, high scores on the A.D.D. screening questionnaire could result from having anxiety, depression, or bipolar problems and/or symptoms. These conditions need to be ruled out before a true diagnosis of Adult A.D.D. can be made.

CONTENTS

SECTION 1: **COMMUNICATION TOOLS**... 1

  ➪ COMMUNICATION SKILLS CHECKLIST........................ 2

  ➪ GOOD COMMUNICATION SKILLS INFORMATION SHEET......... 5

  ➪ SIX WAYS WE COMMUNICATE WITHOUT WORDS
      INFORMATION SHEET.................................... 10

  ➪ EXPRESSING YOUR THOUGHTS AND FEELINGS WORKSHEET... 11

  ➪ OPEN AND CLOSED QUESTIONS WORKSHEET................ 14

  ➪ TURNING COMPLAINTS INTO REQUESTS WORKSHEET........ 17

SECTION 2: **CONFLICT TOOLS**.. 21

  ➪ DIRTY FIGHTING TACTICS INVENTORY...................... 22

  ➪ DIFFERENCES OF OPINION QUESTIONNAIRE................. 26

  ➪ CONFLICT INTERACTION PATTERNS QUESTIONNAIRE........ 29

  ➪ CONFLICT MANAGEMENT STYLES QUESTIONNAIRE.......... 33

  ➪ COUPLES' PROBLEM AND CONFLICT INVENTORY............. 37

  ➪ TIME-OUT SKILLS INFORMATION SHEET AND
      TIME-OUT CONTRACT WORKSHEET....................... 39

⇨ FOUR-STEP PROBLEM-SOLVING PROCEDURE
INFORMATION SHEET AND WORKSHEET. 45

⇨ NEGATIVE REACTION WORKSHEET FOR CONFLICT. 51

⇨ FOUR WAYS TO HELP CREATE POSITIVE SELF-TALK AND
POSITIVE MENTAL PICTURES INFORMATION SHEET. 52

⇨ POSITIVE COUNTER-STATEMENT AND PICTURES
WORKSHEET FOR REDUCING CONFLICT. 53

SECTION 3: **ANGER AND DOMESTIC VIOLENCE TOOLS.** 55

⇨ ANGER INVENTORY. 56

⇨ DOMESTIC VIOLENCE RISK ASSESSMENT INVENTORY. 60

⇨ ATTITUDE CHECKLIST FOR ANGER AND VIOLENCE. 65

⇨ FIVE TYPES OF DOMESTIC ABUSE CHECKLIST. 68

⇨ EARLY WARNING SIGNS IN ANGRY SITUATIONS
INFORMATION SHEET AND WORKSHEET. 71

⇨ ANGER MANAGING ATTITUDE WORKSHEET. 76

⇨ THE ADVANTAGES AND DISADVANTAGES OF ANGER
WORKSHEET. 80

⇨ SIX TYPES OF HOT THOUGHTS THAT ESCALATE ANGER
AND UPSET INFORMATION SHEET. 82

⇨ PREPARING FOR AND HANDLING ANGRY SITUATIONS
INFORMATION SHEET...................................... 84

⇨ EIGHT CHARACTERISTICS OF ABUSIVE HOMES
INFORMATION SHEET...................................... 87

⇨ EIGHT IMPACTS OF CHILDHOOD ABUSE
ON PERSON AS AN ADULT INFORMATION SHEET.............. 89

SECTION 4: **DEPRESSION TOOLS**.................................. 91

⇨ DEPRESSION INVENTORY..................................... 92

⇨ BIPOLAR QUESTIONNAIRE.................................... 96

⇨ DEPRESSED THINKING IS DEPRESSING
INFORMATION SHEET...................................... 98

⇨ 16 WAY TO RE-EVALUATE WHAT YOU SAY TO YOURSELF
INFORMATION SHEET..................................... 101

⇨ NEGATIVE REACTION WORKSHEET FOR DEPRESSION......... 103

⇨ FOUR WAYS TO HELP CREATE POSITIVE SELF-TALK AND
POSITIVE MENTAL PICTURES INFORMATION SHEET.......... 104

⇨ POSITIVE COUNTER-STATEMENTS AND PICTURES
WORKSHEET FOR REDUCING DEPRESSION................... 105

⇨ QUESTIONS TO IDENTIFY POSITIVES AND STRENGTHS........ 106

⇨ IDENTIFICATION AND RANKING OF PLEASURABLE EVENTS
WORKSHEET... 107

⇨ POSSIBLE ACTIVITIES TO IMPROVE DEPRESSION
INFORMATION SHEET. 108

⇨ ACTIVITY SCHEDULE FOR THIS WEEK WORKSHEET. 111

SECTION 5: **ANXIETY TOOLS**. 113

⇨ A MODEL AND DESCRIPTION OF THE FACTORS WHICH
LEAD TO AND MAINTAIN ANXIETY PROBLEMS
INFORMATION SHEET. 114

⇨ A SUMMARY OF SIX TYPES OF ANXIETY PROBLEMS
INFORMATION SHEET. 119

⇨ EXAMPLES OF NEGATIVE AND POSITIVE THINKING FOR
SIX TYPES OF ANXIETY PROBLEMS INFORMATION SHEET. . . . 122

⇨ ANXIETY INVENTORY. 127

⇨ IDENTIFYING CURRENT TRIGGERS WORKSHEET. 133

⇨ ANXIETY REACTION WORKSHEET. 134

⇨ TRAUMA REACTION WORKSHEET. 135

⇨ 16 WAYS TO RE-EVALUATE WHAT YOU SAY TO YOURSELF
INFORMATION SHEET. 136

⇨ FOUR WAYS TO CREATE POSITIVE SELF-TALK AND
POSITIVE MENTAL PICTURES INFORMATION SHEET. 138

⇨ POSITIVE COUNTER-STATEMENTS AND PICTURES
WORKSHEET FOR REDUCING ANXIETY. 139

SECTION 6: **STRESS TOOLS**. 141

⇨ EXTERNAL STRESS TEST. 142

⇨ INTERNAL STRESS TEST. 145

⇨ 42 NEGATIVE CONSEQUENCES OF STRESS CHECKLIST. 147

SECTION 7: **SUBSTANCE ABUSE AND ADDICTION TOOLS**. 149

⇨ PERSONAL RISK PROFILE FOR ADDICTION QUESTIONNAIRE. . . 150

⇨ ALCOHOL SELF-ASSESSMENT QUESTIONNAIRE. 152

⇨ ALCOHOL AND DRUG INFORMATION SHEET. 154

⇨ TWENTY-ONE QUESTIONS TO ASSESS SEX ADDICTION INFORMATION SHEET. 159

⇨ SEXUAL ADDICTION INFORMATION SHEET. 161

SECTION 8: **TOOLS FOR OTHER RELATIONSHIP PROBLEMS**. 163

⇨ INTIMACY QUESTIONNAIRE. 164

⇨ THREE TYPES OF INTIMACY PROBLEMS INFORMATION SHEET. 172

⇨ JEALOUSY QUESTIONNAIRE. 177

- JEALOUSY PROBLEMS INFORMATION SHEET. 180
- INDEX OF RELATIONSHIP SATISFACTION CHECKLIST. 184
- ROMANTIC LOVE BELIEFS QUESTIONNAIRE. 185
- ADULT ATTACHMENT STYLE QUESTIONNAIRE. 188

SECTION 9: **TOOLS FOR OTHER INDIVIDUAL PROBLEMS**. 193

- NEGATIVE SELF-BELIEFS QUESTIONNAIRE. 194
- NEGATIVE REACTION WORKSHEET FOR SELF-BELIEFS. 201
- 16 WAYS TO RE-EVALUATE WHAT YOU SAY TO YOURSELF INFORMATION SHEET. 202
- FOUR WAYS TO HELP CREATE POSITIVE SELF-TALK AND POSITIVE MENTAL PICTURES INFORMATION SHEET. 204
- POSITIVE COUNTER-STATEMENTS AND PICTURES WORKSHEET FOR NEGATIVE SELF-BELIEFS. 205
- SEVEN TYPES OF COGNITIVE DISTORTIONS INFORMATION SHEET. 206
- ADULT A.D.D. SCREENING QUESTIONNAIRE. 210
- ADULT A.D.D. SIGNS AND SYMPTOMS INFORMATION SHEET. . 212
- PERSONAL AND RELATIONSHIP GOALS WORKSHEET. 214
- A SUMMARY OF SIX MAJOR PERSONALITY DISORDERS INFORMATION SHEET. 216

SECTION 1:

COMMUNICATION TOOLS

Clyde M. Feldman, Ph.D.

COMMUNICATION SKILLS CHECKLIST

Please rate yourself on the communication skills below in four areas. Check one of the boxes below (1,2,3,4,5) for each skill to rate how well you use that skill.

	NOT SO WELL				VERY WELL
LISTENING & UNDERSTANDING	1	2	3	4	5
I make an effort to be physically and mentally ready to listen, and pay attention without distractions.					
I listen without interrupting the speaker.					
I tell the speaker, in my own words, what I understand them to be saying.					
I ask the other person what they feel.					
I listen without constantly trying to fix the problem or constantly giving advice.					
I let the speaker talk without changing the topic, tuning them out, or leaving.					
I ask questions to get more information.					
I accept that the other person may have a different opinion than mine and that they are not "Right" or "Wrong".					

EXPRESSING POSITIVES	1	2	3	4	5
I show my affection and caring in words.					
I give praise and compliments.					
I express my appreciation without adding reminders of dissatisfaction.					

TALKING ABOUT FEELINGS	1	2	3	4	5
I put my feelings into words.					
I talk about ME and MY feelings, not just about the other person and what they did.					
I talk about issues that are happening now, rather than bringing up the past.					
I talk about a range of different feelings.					

EXPRESSING NEGATIVE FEELINGS	1	2	3	4	5
I express my negative feelings without stewing over them.					
I focus my negative comments on the other person's ACTIONS, rather than on their character or personality.					
I express my negative feelings without verbal attacks, threats, or intimidation.					
I accept and talk about MY part in problems, rather than blaming the other person for everything.					

MAKING REQUESTS	1	2	3	4	5
I make requests of the other person without waiting until I get all worked up.					
I say "*I would like*" not "*You should*".					
I tell the other person what I want them to do MORE OF, instead of complaining about what they should STOP doing.					
I express my appreciation for positive steps the other person has taken toward doing what I requested.					

INTERPRETATION

The checklist does not have a score, but is meant to help individuals identify and clarify the specific communication skills they need to develop and use in relationships. Skills rated "1" or "2" should be the primary focus for improvement. Skills rated "3" are reasonably good, but could be enhanced.

Adapted and Expanded from P. H. Neidig & D.H. Friedman, 1984

GOOD COMMUNICATION SKILLS

CREATING THE RIGHT CONDITIONS TO TALK

- Tell the other person that it is important that you talk to them.

- Don't plan to talk when one of you is too tired, too hot, too angry, or is intoxicated.

- Decide when and where to talk (home, park, restaurant) so that both people feel comfortable and not frightened, and there are no major distractions. (T.V., stereo, telephone, kids)

- Practice mentally ahead of time what you want to say and how to say it.

- Talk sitting down rather than standing up.

- Realize that If the other person is abusive, you can decide to end the talk and only talk with them after they have calmed down.

ATTENDING

- Be mentally ready to concentrate on what they are saying.

- Sit reasonably close to each other and look at the person eye-to-eye.

- Show with your body language and voice tone that you are really involved and really want to listen.

- Listen carefully, even if you don't agree.

FOLLOWING AND ENCOURAGING

- Nod your head.

- Ask "open" questions (What? How? Where? When? Why?) to get more information when you're unclear, confused, or want to help the speaker be more specific.

- Say things that tell the person "I hear you" and "I want you to keep Talking". (For example: "Uh-huh", "I know what you mean", "Really?", "Yeh", "Right", "I didn't know that", "I don't understand")

- Check out your assumptions... they may be WRONG!

UNDERSTANDING

- In your own words, repeat and summarize the important points you just heard.... especially their feelings.

- Try not to be defensive or counterattack.

- Put yourself in the other person's shoes.

- You can disagree and still be a good listener. Just hearing what they say as their opinion, different then yours, but NOT stupid, wrong, ridiculous, or crazy.

EXPRESSING NEGATIVE FEELINGS

- Figure out what ALL your feelings are, not just feelings of ANGER.

- Don't assume that just because the other person knows you, they should be able to read your thoughts and your feelings.

- Don't use name calling, insults, threats, and attacks to express yourself. These are dirty fighting tactics that get the other person to retaliate, to escalate, and to get revenge.

- Express your negative feelings IN WORDS, not by the tone in your voice, or the expression on your face, or the "silent treatment".

- Express your negative feelings promptly, rather than holding them in.

- Handle criticism by not taking it so personally and by finding some way to agree with some point the other person is making.

- Don't bring up the past. Stay focused on the "here and now" issues.

- Talk about your feelings and thoughts, not just what that other person did.

- Take turns talking and listening.

USE THE FORMULA:

"WHEN YOU _____ (DO OR SAY), I FEEL _____ BECAUSE _____".

Clyde M. Feldman, Ph.D.

MAKING POSITIVE REQUESTS

- Make requests, NOT DEMANDS.

- Request what you would like them TO DO INSTEAD, not what they're doing wrong.

- Help them to understand how this will help you and help the relationship.

- Know that the other person always has a choice.

- Reward and compliment them for making positive attempts at doing what you requested.

USE THE FORMULA:

" I'D REALLY LIKE IT IF   YOU WOULD _____ BECAUSE _____ ".
" I'D APPRECIATE IT IF   YOU WOULD _____ BECAUSE _____ ".
" IT WOULD HELP ME IF   YOU WOULD _____ BECAUSE _____ ".
" IT WOULD BE GREAT IF   YOU WOULD _____ BECAUSE _____ ".

GIVING APPRECIATIONS AND COMPLIMENTS

- Don't assume that because you gave a compliment ONCE it never needs to be given again. You can't give too many compliments.

- Catch them in the act of DOING SOMETHING RIGHT.

- Sharing positive feelings of affection, caring, and appreciation helps break the cycle of hearing only criticism and hurtful messages.

- Make sure what you say is the truth. Don't B.S. the other person.

- DON'T FALL INTO THE "CANCELLED-OUT COMPLIMENT" TRAP!

FOR EXAMPLE:

"I love you, when you're not being an asshole."
"You're a great cook, even though you hardly do it anymore."

• SOME EXAMPLE POSITIVE QUALITIES TO COMPLIMENT ARE:

COMFORTABLE AROUND DIFFERENT TYPES OF PEOPLE	BELIEVES THEY AND/OR OTHERS CAN CHANGE	GOTTEN THROUGH DIFFICULT TIMES
CAN SEE THEIR OWN FAULTS	WILLING TO HELP OTHERS	CAN BE INDEPENDENT
MAKES GOOD DECISIONS	A HARD WORKER	PLANS AHEAD
NON-JUDGEMENTAL	GOOD SENSE OF HUMOR	TAKES THE INITIATIVE
TOLERATES FRUSTRATION	EXPRESSES FEELINGS	BONDS WITH OTHERS
CAN FOLLOW OTHERS' LEAD	GIVES AS WELL AS TAKES	CONSIDERATE
STRONG CULTURAL IDENTITY	STRONG SPIRITUAL BELIEFS	STAYS OPTIMISTIC
PERSISTENT / DETERMINED	CAREFUL	LOYAL
TRUSTING	DEPENDABLE	TOLERANT
GENEROUS	STABLE	DOES NOT BLAME
LIKED BY PEOPLE	KIND AND CARING	FRIENDLY
ORGANIZED	ASSERTIVE	EMPATHETIC
SMART	SELF-CONFIDENT	INTERESTING
INSIGHTFUL / PERCEPTIVE	STICKS UP FOR ONESELF	FUNNY
REALISTIC	A CRITICAL THINKER	WANTS TO CHANGE
HANDLES CRITICISM WELL	DETAIL-ORIENTED	FLEXIBLE / ADAPTABLE
COOPERATIVE	CAN BE PART OF A TEAM	ETHICAL
NOT REVENGEFUL	UNDERSTANDING	CREATIVE / ARTISTIC
GOOD MOTHER/FATHER	PROBLEM-SOLVER	GOOD COOK
WILLING TO SACRIFICE	RESPONSIBLE	HAS GOALS
SEES THINGS FROM OTHERS' POINT OF VIEW	KNOWS WHEN TO BACK OFF	KNOWS HOW TO BE SPONTANEOUS
KNOWS HOW TO BE A FRIEND	IS EMOTIONALLY SAFE	CAN BE TRUSTED

© Clyde M. Feldman, 1994

SIX WAYS WE COMMUNICATE WITHOUT WORDS

Remember that in close relationships what you say *without words* often carries more weight than what you say *in words*. It also changes the meaning of what you say in words. The six non-verbal "channels" of communication below can send a positive or a negative message. What message are you sending?

NON-VERBAL CHANNEL	EXAMPLE BEHAVIORS
FACIAL EXPRESSION ⇨	Angry look. Frown. Smile. Cry.
VOICE TONE ⇨	Loud voice. Soft voice. Sarcastic tone. Irritated tone. Tender tone.
EYE CONTACT ⇨	Look in their eyes. Look away. Stare at something or at the floor while someone's talking. Roll your eyes.
BODY LANGUAGE ⇨	Give the finger. Throw something. Turn your body toward them. Shake your head. Make a fist at someone. Turn your whole body away from someone while they're talking.
DISTANCE ⇨	Stand or sit far away or close. Walk away. Stay in another room. Get in someone's face. Follow someone from room to room.
TOUCH ⇨	Slap. Hug. Pull hair. Hold their hand.

© Clyde M. Feldman, 1994

EXPRESSING YOUR THOUGHTS AND FEELINGS

When something's bothering you, or you have a disagreement or conflict, there are TWO kinds of messages you can use to express your thoughts and feelings: <u>YOU MESSAGES</u> and <u>I MESSAGES</u>.

YOU MESSAGE

- Attacks the other person with name calling, insults, and threats.
- Makes the other person use the same attack messages back.
- Makes the other person feel defensive and criticized.
- Escalates the problem into a "battle" or a "war".
- Doesn't let the other person know what they should do differently.
- Hurts the other person deep-down, and they begin to lose trust in the relationship.
- Decreases closeness, understanding, caring, and intimacy.

EXAMPLES:

"You live like a pig!"
"You're selfish and inconsiderate!"
"Why can't you stop being an jerk?"
"Who the hell do you think you are?"

"You're always in a bad mood!"
"You expect everyone to be perfect"
"You treat me like dirt!"
"You're a lying son of a bitch!"

I MESSAGE

- Talks about <u>me</u> not <u>them</u>, so the other person doesn't feel so defensive.
- Focuses on their specific behavior, not their attitudes or character.
- Lets you express your thoughts and feelings instead of holding them in.
- Helps the other person to understand you.
- Helps motivate the other person to make some changes.
- Increases closeness, understanding, caring, and intimacy.

I MESSAGES USE THE FORMULA:

WHEN YOU_____ (DO OR SAY), I FEEL _____ , BECAUSE _____

EXAMPLES:

"When you question me about everything I do and everywhere I go, I feel uptight and criticized because it feels like you're the parent and I'm the child".

"When you make jokes about getting back together with your boyfriend, I feel insecure and hurt, because you've cheated on me before and I don't feel like I can trust you".

"When you hit our daughter, I feel hatred toward you, because you make me chose between my love for you and my love for my baby".

EXAMPLES OF TURNING <u>YOU</u> STATEMENTS ➠ <u>I</u> STATEMENTS

You: "You always put me down."
I: **"When you criticize me in front of our friends, I feel hurt and embarrassed, because I'm already feeling down on myself about being out of work".**

You: "You're so damn irresponsible".
I: **"When you're an hour late picking me up and don't call, I feel stupid and uncared for because it reminds me of what my father used to do when he was drinking".**

You: "Why do you always avoid the problem?"
I: **"When you won't talk to me for a week, I feel frustrated, because I can't solve our problems without you being part of the solution".**

You: "You're a selfish son-of-a-bitch?"
I: **"When you leave me with the baby and go out with all your friends, I feel trapped and unappreciated, because I work hard every day and I don't get to relax".**

ACTIVITY 1: The first step in using I statements is RECOGNIZING WHAT PROBLEMS YOU SEE IN YOUR RELATIONSHIP WITH THE OTHER PERSON. List one *minor* problem or pet peeve and two *major* problems with someone who you get upset with.

A MINOR PROBLEM IS: _____

A MAJOR PROBLEM IS: _____

_____

A MAJOR PROBLEM IS: _____

_____

ACTIVITY 2: TRY CHANGING THE *YOU MESSAGES* BELOW INTO *I MESSAGES*.
Imagine that you're in a situation where you have made the statements below. Then use the formula (WHEN YOU ____ (DO OR SAY), I FEEL ___, BECAUSE ____) to help you turn what you might be thinking and feeling into an I MESSAGE.

You Message: You piss me off!

I Message: _____

_____

You Message: You're such an idiot!

I Message: _____

_____

You Message: You always think you're right and everybody else is wrong!

I Message: _____

_____

You Message: You don't give a shit about me!

I Message: _____

_____

You Message: (write in one of your own) _____

I Message: _____

_____

© Clyde M. Feldman, 1994

OPEN AND CLOSED QUESTIONS

An important communication skill is *asking questions* to get more information about how the other person is feeling and what they are thinking. There are two types of questions: **OPEN** and **CLOSED**. CLOSED questions are like true/false or multiple choice questions, while OPEN questions are like essay question.

A CLOSED QUESTION:
- Makes the other person feel defensive.
- Suggests that you already know what the "right" answer is.
- Shuts down the conversation.
- Limits the amount of information you will get.
- Requires short, simple answers like "yes" or "no".

AN OPEN QUESTION:
- Increases closeness, understanding, and intimacy.
- Makes the other person feel like you really want to understand them.
- Keeps the conversation going.
- Increases the amount of information you will get.
- Gives the person a chance to really talk about themselves fully.

EXAMPLES OF MAKING CLOSED QUESTIONS ➟ OPEN QUESTIONS

Closed: "I know you were at the bar last night, weren't you?"
Open: "Where did you go last night?"

Closed: "Are you angry at me?"
Open: "How does it make you feel when that happens?"

Closed: "You're just doing this to mess with my mind, aren't you?"
Open: "Why did you react to me that way? What going on inside you?"

Closed: "Do you want to go tonight or not?"
Open: "How do you feel about being out with them tonight?"

Closed: "Did you have a good trip to the mountains?"
Open: "How'd your trip to the mountains go?"

ACTIVITY 1: CHECK THE QUESTIONS BELOW WHICH ARE <u>OPEN</u> QUESTIONS?

___ How was your day?

___ You don't think I'm selfish, do you?

___ Do you think John's lying?

___ What do you think of our president?

ACTIVITY 2: IMAGINE THAT YOU'RE IN A SITUATION WHERE YOU HAVE ASKED THE CLOSED QUESTIONS BELOW. THEN TRY MAKING THOSE *CLOSED* QUESTIONS INTO *OPEN* QUESTIONS. REMEMBER, THERE ARE MANY POSSIBLE OPEN QUESTIONS FOR EACH OF THE CLOSED QUESTIONS BELOW.

Closed: Are you happy about the way it turned out?
Open: _____
_____

Closed: You don't really believe that do you?
Open: _____
_____

Closed: You're pissed because I didn't call, aren't you?
Open: _____
_____

Closed: You're all upset about your mother again, right?
Open: _____
_____

Closed: Do you want to go to counseling with me or not?
Open: _____
_____

Closed: I know you've been thinking about cheating on me, haven't you?
Open: _____
_____

Closed: I don't like the son-of-a-bitch, do you?
Open: _____
_____

Closed: Did you have a good time yesterday?
Open: _____
_____

Closed: (Write in one of your own closed questions) _____
_____

Open: _____
_____

Closed: (Write another one of your own) _____
_____

Open: _____
_____

© Clyde M. Feldman, 1994

TURNING COMPLAINTS INTO REQUESTS

If you want things to change in your relationship, **YOU** will have to change! You might be saying to yourself right now "But it's not me that causing the problem. Even if **I** changed, _____ would still be doing the same thing." Well, there are two ways that **YOU** can change. Change *yourself* and change *the way you try to get other people to change THEIR behavior*.

COMPLAINING TRIES TO CHANGE PEOPLE BY

- ***Demanding*** that they should.
- Telling them what they're doing **wrong**.
- Not telling them **in words**, but only with our voice tone, facial expressions, or avoiding/walking out on them.
- Constantly **repeating the same complaints** and gripes over and over until they hopefully "get it".

Examples:

"Don't be such a slob, God damn it!"
"You never show me any affection!"
"You never want to talk things over!"
"Why are you always complaining?"
"Don't insult me in front of my friends!"

"Stop treating me like a child!"
"Don't be so narrow-mined!"
"Stop nagging me all the time!"
"Don't try to provoke me!"
"Shut the hell up!"

TURNING COMPLAINTS INTO REQUESTS MEANS BEING

- **PROMPT** — Make requests when they **FIRST** become an issue, rather than silently holding them inside.

- **POSITIVE** — Suggest what you want the person to **DO MORE OF**, instead of what they should do less of or stop doing.

- **SPECIFIC** — Focus on **SPECIFIC** behavior, not their attitudes or character.

- **REWARDING** — Let the other person know why it will be positive for you and how it will help you. Reward and compliment even small steps and attempts they make at doing what you requested. Help them **WANT** to help you.

- **ASSERTIVE** You have the **RIGHT TO ASK** regardless of what the other person decides to do. This is different than being **SUBMISSIVE** and it's different than being **AGGRESSIVE** and getting your way by using threats, humiliation, and force.

SUCCESSFUL REQUESTS USE THE FORMULA:

> **I'D LIKE IT IF YOU WOULD (DO OR SAY) _____ , BECAUSE _____**

EXAMPLES OF TURNING COMPLAINTS ➨ REQUESTS

Complaint: "Don't put me down all the time."
Request: **"It would be great if you would compliment me once in a while for working hard because I would feel appreciated for contributing to the family."**

Complaint: "Stop treating me like a child."
Request: **"I would appreciate it if you would ask what I think about important decisions because I would feel like you respect me and value my opinion."**

Complaint: "You never listen to me"
Request: **"I'd really like it if you would take some time and ask me how my day was. It would help me feel like you understand me more and also help me not feel so stressed out about work.**

ACTIVITY 1: The first step in making successful requests is KNOWING WHAT YOU *WANT AND NEED MORE OF* - from who, and in what situations. You may want MORE support, attention, listening, respect, time to yourself, forgiveness, answers, understanding, money (a raise).

1) I Want: _____

   From: _____ In The Situation: _____

2) I Want: _____

   From: _____ In The Situation: _____

ACTIVITY 2: Image that you're in a situation where you have made the statements below. Then try changing these COMPLAINTS AND DEMANDS into REQUESTS for change. Use the formula (I'd like it if you would ___ because ___) to help you.

Complaint: Stop being such a selfish fool!
Request: _____
_____

Complaint: Stop trying to change me!
Request: _____
_____

Complaint: You never appreciate anything I ever do!
Request: _____
_____

Complaint: Don't criticize me all the time!
Request: _____
_____

Complaint: (Write in one of your own) _____
_____

Request: _____
_____

© Clyde M. Feldman, 1994

SECTION 2:

CONFLICT TOOLS

Clyde M. Feldman, Ph.D.

Dirty Fighting Techniques

Indicate how often you have used each of the dirty fighting techniques below during conflicts, disagreements, or arguments with a partner or spouse.

0= Never   1= Rarely   2= Sometimes   3= Often

____ **Timing.** Pick the right time to begin an argument. Late at night, during a favorite TV show, after several drinks, or just before your partner has to leave for work are options. As a general rule, look for the time your partner least expects it, or is least able to respond.

____ **Escalating.** Move quickly from the issue, to the questioning of personality, to wondering whether it is worth the effort to stay together (issue to personality to relationship). Interpret your partner's shortcomings as evidence of bad faith, and the impossibility of a happy relationship.

____ **Brown Bagging.** Try to list as many problems in as much detail as possible. Don't stick to the original issue, but rather throw in all the problems you can't think of. Don't limit yourself to the present. If your partner can't remember the offense, so much the better.

____ **Over-generalizing.** Use words like "always" and "never" as in "you are always late." This is likely to distract your partner into discussing the over-generalization rather than the issue and insure further misunderstandings.

____ **Cross-complaining.** Respond to any complaint your partner may raise with one of your own. For example, "Me late? Why, if it weren't for the fact that you never have any clean clothes for me..." If done properly you can balance complaint against complaint forever.

____ **Crucializing.** Exaggerate the importance of the issue with statements such as "If you really loved us, you would have never done it in the first place" or "This proves that you don't care." Never concede that an issue is not absolutely critical and in need of immediate resolution.

____ **Asking Why.** "Why didn't you clean up?" or "Why were you late?" will imply that there must be something terribly wrong with your partner and that something more than a simple problem that might easily be resolved is at issue.

_____ **Blaming**. Make it clear that fault lies entirely with your partner and that once again you are simply the innocent victim. Don't admit that your behavior plays any part in the difficulty. Make sure that your partner realizes that you will not change first.

_____ **Pulling Rank.** Rather than depend on the merits of your argument, pull rank by reminding your partner that you make more money, have more education, are older or younger, or are wiser and more experienced in such matters. Anything that will enhance your status at your partner's expense should be considered.

_____ **Not Listening, Dominating.** Any time you appear to be listening you run the risk of suggesting that you value your partner's opinion. Consider talking while your partner is trying to talk, pretending to read, or falling asleep.

_____ **Listing Injustices.** This is a great morale builder. By reciting every slight, injustice, or inequity you have suffered in the relationship, you will experience a renewed sense of self-righteousness. You can use this approach to justify almost any activity you have wanted to engage in. For example, "Since you bought that dress, now I can buy a new car."

_____ **Labeling.** By labeling somebody in a negative manner, you can create the impression that that person is totally at fault. Psychological labels, such as "immature," "neurotic," "paranoid," or "alcoholic," are particularly effective in obscuring issues where you may be vulnerable.

_____ **Mind-Reading.** By deciding that you know the real reason why someone is acting in a certain way, you can avoid having to debate issues. For example, "You only said that to set me up" or "You don't really feel that way" are particularly effective.

_____ **Fortune-Telling.** Predicting the future can save you the effort of really trying to resolve problems. "You will never change" or "It would be easy for me to change, but you wouldn't live up to it" are statements that can protect you from having to make any effort at all.

_____ **Being Sarcastic.** This is a great way of saying something without having to take responsibility for it. If you can say, "You're so smart..." just right, you can imply that your partner is stupid and deny that you said it at the same time.

____ **Avoiding Responsibility.** Although not a very elegant tactic, saying "I don't remember" can bring the discussion to an abrupt halt. Alcohol or fatigue can serve the same purpose, as in "I must have been drunk."

____ **Leaving.** No problem is so big or important that it can't be ignored. Walk out of the room, leave home, or just refuse to talk. Sometimes just threatening to leave can accomplish the same end without the inconvenience involved in actually leaving.

____ **Rejecting Compromise.** Don't back down. Why settle for compromise when with a little luck you can really devastate your partner (and destroy the relationship). Stick with the "one winner" philosophy.

____ **Personalizing.** Anybody can resolve a conflict by sticking to the issue. Shift to personalities and you should be able to generate enough defensiveness to keep the conflict going forever. For example, if you happen to be upset by the fact that the room wasn't straightened, start with "You slob..." to suggest that it is your partner's existence and not behavior that is at question.

____ **Playing The Martyr.** If timed properly, this tactic can completely disorient the opposition. "You're right dear, I am hopeless" can stop your partner cold. An example of a less subtle form is, "How could you say that after all I've done for you?" An extreme form is to threaten to kill yourself if your partner doesn't shape up.

____ **Using Money.** If you made as much money as...", or "When you make as much as I do, then you can have an opinion," are old favorites.

____ **Using Children.** "If you spent more time with them, they wouldn't be failing" or "Do you want them to grow up like you?" can always be used unless you are fortunate enough to have perfect children.

____ **Using Relatives.** "When you do that, you are just like your mother" can be used to undermine confidence.

____ **Giving Advice.** By telling people how to act, think, and feel, you can maintain a position of superiority while insisting that you are only trying to be helpful.

____ **Getting Even**. Don't settle for a compromise or an apology. Hold grudges for as long as possible. Find ways of getting back at your partner or punishing them.

____ **Being Inconsistent**. Keep your partner off balance by changing your position. Try complaining that your partner never talks to you and then ignore whatever your partner may have to say.

____ **Others**. This list should only be considered suggestive of the range of tactics to be drawn from. With practice and creativity, you should be able to come up with numerous innovations.

SCORING

COUNT UP THE NUMBER OF ITEMS THAT YOU PUT A "2" FOR = _____

COUNT UP THE NUMBER OF ITEMS THAT YOU PUT A "3" FOR = _____

NO 3's AND NO 2's................................. **= EXTREMELY FAIR "FIGHTER"**

NO 3's AND UP TO THREE 2's.................... **= PRETTY FAIR "FIGHTER"**

NO 3's AND FOUR OR MORE 2's................ **= BE CAREFUL, THIS CAN BE TROUBLE**

ONE OR TWO 3's...................................... **= YOU CAN BE A DIRTY "FIGHTER"**

THREE OR MORE 3's................................ **= YOU CAN BE A VERY DIRTY "FIGHTER"**

Clyde M. Feldman, Ph.D.

DIFFERENCES OF OPINION QUESTIONNAIRE

The statements below describe different areas in which you and a partner may have had differences of opinion Think about either a CURRENT or a PAST relationship and for each of the statements below, please circle a number from 0 to 6 which means the degree to which you and that person have THE SAME OR DIFFERENT OPINIONS about various things.

0	1	2	3	4	5	6
No Difference Of Opinion						Extremely Different Opinions

For example, if you had EXTREMELY DIFFERENT OPINIONS about how to discipline the kids, you would circle 6. If you had NO DIFFERENCE OF OPINION about how to discipline the kids, you would circle 0. If you had somewhat different opinions, you would circle a number between 1 and 5 that fits.

1. Difference of opinion about what money is spent on, how much money is spent, or how money is managed. 0 1 2 3 4 5 6

2. Difference of opinion about major household chores and tasks. 0 1 2 3 4 5 6

3. Difference of opinion about when we eat, where we eat, and what we eat. 0 1 2 3 4 5 6

4. Difference of opinion about the way one of us dresses, how one of us looks, or personal hygiene. 0 1 2 3 4 5 6

5. Difference of opinion about the way we should handle problems between us. 0 1 2 3 4 5 6

6. Difference of opinion about the use of criticism. 0 1 2 3 4 5 6

7. Difference of opinion about the way feelings get talked about. 0 1 2 3 4 5 6

8. Difference of opinion about giving compliments, praise, or appreciations. 0 1 2 3 4 5 6

9. Difference of opinion about getting the other person's attention. 0 1 2 3 4 5 6

10. Difference of opinion about what being romantic means. 0 1 2 3 4 5 6

11. Difference of opinion about dealing with family members or relatives. 0 1 2 3 4 5 6

12. Difference of opinion about the frequency of sexual activities. 0 1 2 3 4 5 6

13. Difference of opinion about the quality of sexual activities. 0 1 2 3 4 5 6

14. Difference of opinion about the use of alcohol or drugs. 0 1 2 3 4 5 6

15. Difference of opinion about work schedules. 0 1 2 3 4 5 6

16. Difference of opinion about job or career choices. 0 1 2 3 4 5 6

17. Difference of opinion about disciplining the children. (if no children, leave blank) 0 1 2 3 4 5 6

18. Difference of opinion about her what we do or where we go with the children. (if no children, leave blank) 0 1 2 3 4 5 6

19. Difference of opinion about how much time we have to ourselves. 0 1 2 3 4 5 6

20. Difference of opinion about the way we spend time alone. 0 1 2 3 4 5 6

21. Difference of opinion about how often we go out socially together, what we do when we go out, or who we're with. 0 1 2 3 4 5 6

22. Difference of opinion about how much time we spend together. 0 1 2 3 4 5 6

23. Difference of opinion about relationships with same-sex friends. 0 1 2 3 4 5 6

24. Difference of opinion about relationships with opposite-sex friends. 0 1 2 3 4 5 6

25. Difference of opinion about taking vacations and trips. 0 1 2 3 4 5 6

26. Difference of opinion about what it means to be a responsible and mature person. 0 1 2 3 4 5 6

27. Difference of opinion about religious beliefs or practices. 0 1 2 3 4 5 6

28. Difference of opinion about our personal values. 0 1 2 3 4 5 6

SCORING

COUNT UP HOW MANY ITEMS YOU CIRCLED 4, 5, OR 6.   YOUR SCORE IS: _____

0-3 =   This suggests that your differences can be frustrating but usually doesn't put intense stress on the relationship bond. Solving these differences depends on your ability to really understand the other person's position, accept some differences, and know how to compromise and negotiate as allies rather than enemies.

4+ =   This suggests that your differences can put intense stress on the relationship bond. There may be major incompatibility problems or problems in understanding the other person's position, accepting some differences, and in compromising and negotiating as allies, not enemies.

Adapted and expanded by Clyde M. Feldman from Weiss, Hops, & Patterson, 1973

CONFLICT INTERACTION PATTERNS QUESTIONNAIRE

This questionnaire is about how you and your partner typically deal with problems in your relationship. Please circle a number from 1 to 7 meaning how likely it is that it happens.

A. WHEN SOME PROBLEM IN THE RELATIONSHIP ARISES:

	Very Unlikely					Very Likely	

1. <u>Mutual Avoidance</u>: We both avoid discussing the problem.
   1 2 3 4 5 6 7

2. <u>Mutual Discussion</u>: We both try to discuss the problem.   1 2 3 4 5 6 7

3. <u>Discussion/Avoidance</u>:
   a) I try to start a discussion, while my partner tries to avoid a discussion.   1 2 3 4 5 6 7

   b) My partner tries to start a discussion, while I try to avoid a discussion.   1 2 3 4 5 6 7

B. DURING AN ARGUMENT OR DISCUSSION OF A RELATIONSHIP PROBLEM:

1. <u>Criticize/Defend</u>:
   a) I criticize, blame, and accuse, while my partner defends themself.   1 2 3 4 5 6 7

   b) My partner criticizes, blames, and accuses, while I defend myself.   1 2 3 4 5 6 7

2. <u>Emotional Expression</u>:
   a) I express my feelings in words to my partner.   1 2 3 4 5 6 7

   b) My partner expresses in words their feelings to me.   1 2 3 4 5 6 7

3. <u>Negotiation</u>:
   a) I offer possible solutions and compromises.   1 2 3 4 5 6 7

   b) My partner offers possible solutions and compromises. 1 2 3 4 5 6 7

4. <u>Demand/Withdraw</u>:
   a) I press, complain, and demand, while my partner withdraws,
      becomes silent, or refuses to discuss the matter further.   1 2 3 4 5 6 7

   b) My partner presses, complains, & demands, while I withdraw,
      become silent, or refuse to discuss the matter further.   1 2 3 4 5 6 7

5. <u>Threaten/Back down</u>:
   a) I threaten my partner with something negative, and they
      ultimately give in or back down.   1 2 3 4 5 6 7

   b) My partner threatens me with something negative,
      and I ultimately give in or back down.   1 2 3 4 5 6 7

6. <u>Pressure/Resist</u>:
   a) I pressure my partner to do something or stop doing
      something, while they resist.   1 2 3 4 5 6 7

   b) My partner pressures me to do something or stop doing
      something, while I resist.   1 2 3 4 5 6 7

7. <u>Verbal Aggression</u>:
   a) I call my partner names, ridicule them, swear at them,
      or attack their character, competence, or appearance.   1 2 3 4 5 6 7

   b) My partner calls me names, ridicules me, swears at me,
      or attacks my character, competence, or appearance.   1 2 3 4 5 6 7

8. <u>Physical Aggression</u>:
   a) I push, shove, slap, hit, scratch, bite, grab, restrain, kick,
      or punch them.   1 2 3 4 5 6 7

   b) My partner pushes, shoves, slaps, hits, scratches, bites,
      grabs, restrains, kicks, or punches me.   1 2 3 4 5 6 7

C. AFTER AN ARGUMENT OR DISCUSSION OF A RELATIONSHIP PROBLEM:

1. <u>Understanding</u>:
   a) I understand my partner's point of view and position.   1 2 3 4 5 6 7

   b) My partner understands my point of view and position.   1 2 3 4 5 6 7

2. a) <u>Mutual Reconciliation</u>: We both feel like we are getting along again and things are back to normal.   1 2 3 4 5 6 7

   b) <u>Reconcile/Withdraw</u>:
   I act like things are back to normal and we're getting along again, while my partner acts distant and withdrawn.   1 2 3 4 5 6 7

   c) My partner acts like things are back to normal and we're getting along again, while I act distant and withdrawn.   1 2 3 4 5 6 7

   d) <u>Mutual Withdraw</u>: We both act distant and withdrawn from each other.   1 2 3 4 5 6 7

3. a) <u>Mutual Resolution</u>: We both feel like the problem has been solved to our mutual liking.   1 2 3 4 5 6 7

   b) <u>Resolved/Nonresolved</u>:
   I feel like the problem has been solved to my liking, but my partner feels like it's not really been solved to their liking.   1 2 3 4 5 6 7

   c) My partner feels like the problem has been solved to their liking, but I feel like it's not really been solved to my liking.   1 2 3 4 5 6 7

4. <u>Withholding</u>:
   a) I withhold support, warmth, attention, sex, etc. from my partner.   1 2 3 4 5 6 7

   b) My partner withholds support, warmth, attention, sex, etc. from me.   1 2 3 4 5 6 7

5. <u>Decision-Making</u>:
   a) I feel like I had as much say in how the problem was going to be solved as I wanted to.   1 2 3 4 5 6 7

   b) My partner feels like they had as much say in how the problem was going to be solved as they wanted to.   1 2 3 4 5 6 7

6. Pressure/Resist:
   a) I pressure my partner to apologize, to admit they were wrong, or to promise to do better, while they resist.   1 2 3 4 5 6 7

   b) My partner pressures me to apologize, admit I was wrong, or promise to do better, while I resist.   1 2 3 4 5 6 7

7. a) <u>Mutually Encouraged</u>: We both feel more hop<u>eful</u> and <u>en</u>couraged about the problem.   1 2 3 4 5 6 7

   b) <u>Mutually Discouraged</u>: We both feel more hopel<u>ess</u> and <u>dis</u>couraged about the problem.   1 2 3 4 5 6 7

   c) <u>Encouraged/Discouraged</u>:
   I feel more hopel<u>ess</u> and <u>dis</u>couraged about the problem, while my partner feels more hop<u>eful</u> and <u>en</u>couraged.   1 2 3 4 5 6 7

   d) My partner feels more hopel<u>ess</u> and <u>dis</u>couraged about the problem, while I feel more hop<u>eful</u> and <u>en</u>couraged.   1 2 3 4 5 6 7

8. Support Seeking:
   a) I seek support from people like friends, family, etc.   1 2 3 4 5 6 7

   b) My partner seeks support from people like friends, family, etc.   1 2 3 4 5 6 7

INTERPRETATION

The questionnaire does not have a score, but is meant to help individuals identify (1) the types of negative, dysfunctional patterns of conflict they use and the extent to which they use these negative patterns, and (2) the extent to which they use positive, healthy patterns of conflict. The healthy patterns identified in the questionnaire are:

A2. MUTUAL DISCUSSION
B2. EMOTIONAL EXPRESSION
B3. NEGOTIATION
C1. UNDERSTANDING
C2. MUTUAL RECONCILIATION
C3. MUTUAL RESOLUTION
C5. DECISION-MAKING
C7. MUTUAL ENCOURAGED
C8. SUPPORT SEEKING

Adapted and Expanded by Clyde M. Feldman from Christensen, 1988

CONFLICT MANAGEMENT STYLES

The 30 items below are about your behavior when you experience disagreements and conflicts with other people. Rate the degree to which each item describes your typical behavior during situations of conflict. This might be with a partner, with friends, or at work. Use the scale:

> 0= I never behave this way
> 1= I seldom behave this way
> 2= I sometimes behave this way
> 3= I often behave this way
> 4= I very often behave this way

_____ 1. I directly confront the other person even if it's uncomfortable for them.

_____ 2. I disregard the existence of a conflict.

_____ 3. I comply with the other person's requests.

_____ 4. I seek a mutually beneficial solution.

_____ 5. I seek a quick middle ground solution.

_____ 6. I engage in a verbal fight when necessary.

_____ 7. I postpone dealing with the issue.

_____ 8. I sacrifice my own wishes for the sake of the other person.

_____ 9. I work closely with the other person to find new and different options.

_____ 10. I give up something or modify something if the other person will do the same.

_____ 11. I find it difficult to stop myself in a heated discussion.

_____ 12. I avoid communicating with the other person.

_____ 13. I give in to the other person for the sake of harmony.

_____ 14. I actively try to get information about the other person's thoughts and feelings.

_____ 15. I "split the difference" with the other person.

_____ 16. I try to win the conflict even though it means that somebody has to lose.

_____ 17. I sidestep the topics that the disagreement is about.

_____ 18. I protect my relationship with the other person rather than wining the conflict.

_____ 19. I explore alternative solutions to the problem that have probably not been tried.

_____ 20. I bargain about things with the other person.

_____ 21. I refuse to back down or compromise when I feel I am right.

_____ 22. I withdraw from the situation if it becomes too confrontational.

_____ 23. I yield to the other person's position.

_____ 24. I attempt to negotiate so that neither person must compromise anything.

_____ 25. I concede some points in order to win other points.

_____ 26. I put pressure on the other person to back down or agree with my position.

_____ 27. I change the topic to avoid confrontation.

_____ 28. I let the other person have his/her way.

_____ 29. I put about equal effort to get my needs met and to help them get their needs met.

_____ 30. I am satisfied with getting "part of the pie".

SCORING:

THERE ARE FIVE DIFFERENT STYLES OR PREFERENCES FOR HANDLING CONFLICT. THEY ARE COMPETING, AVOIDING, ACCOMMODATING, COLLABORATING, AND COMPROMISING. FIND YOUR SCORE FOR THE ITEMS IN THE COLUMNS BELOW. THEN ADD UP YOUR SCORES IN EACH COLUMN BELOW.

Competing	Avoiding	Accommodating	Collaborating	Compromising
1. _____	2. _____	3. _____	4. _____	5. _____
6. _____	7. _____	8. _____	9. _____	10. _____
11. _____	12. _____	13. _____	14. _____	15. _____
16. _____	17. _____	18. _____	19. _____	20. _____
21. _____	22. _____	23. _____	24. _____	25. _____
26. _____	27. _____	28. _____	29. _____	30. _____
Total _____	Tot _____	Tot _____	Tot _____	Tot _____

YOUR HIGHEST TOTAL SCORE TO YOUR LOWEST TOTAL SCORE REPRESENTS YOUR MOST LIKELY USED STYLE/PREFERENCE TO YOUR LEAST LIKELY USED STYLE/PREFERENCE FOR HANDLING CONFLICT.

MOST LIKELY TO USE   _____

2ND PREFERENCE   _____

3RD PREFERENCE   _____

4TH PREFERENCE   _____

LEAST LIKELY TO USE   _____

DESCRIPTION OF THE FIVE STYLES/PREFERENCES

1. *COMPETING* - **I WIN - YOU LOSE STYLE**. One emphasizes their own goals and needs and pursues their view without taking into account or adjusting for the opinions or needs of the other. **Disadvantages:** It discounts the other's good ideas; it personally attacks the other position in order to stay a winner; it forces the other to choose your way which isn't often the best solution; the other is not tied-in to that choice. **Advantages:** Someone may need to take charge when things are deadlocked; someone takes responsibility for doing something.

2. *AVOIDING* - **I LOSE - YOU WIN STYLE**. One avoids conflict and sidesteps participating by withdrawing or changing the subject - thereby pursuing neither your own or the others' goals. **Disadvantages:** It conveys a message of not caring; it puts the problem on the back burner, it reinforces the discomfort and fear of dealing with disagreement- can't cope unless there is harmony. **Advantages:** It may give person more time to think and plan.

3. *ACCOMMODATING* - **I LOSE - YOU WIN STYLE**. One gives in to the others' views/desires and chooses to sacrifice their own personal needs. **Disadvantages:** You give up adding your input; you may become resentful or get even; you may be too focused on wanting to be liked. **Advantages:** It helps maintain relationships by putting the relational over the task goals; it may minimize harmful interpersonal consequences.

4. **_COLLABORATING_ - I WIN - YOU WIN STYLE.** One emphasizes reaching their own goals but also emphasizes the other person's goals. **Disadvantages:** It requires both people to be very involved in understanding their positions and what each needs; you have to find creative, unique solutions which is time consuming. **Advantages:** It gives both sides a voice; it reinforces the idea that both parties are equally valued; it examines issues thoroughly; it maximizes the probability that the problem is really solved, and that both people will be motivated to follow through with the decisions made.

5. **_COMPROMISING_ - I WIN SOME AND LOSE SOME - YOU WIN SOME AND LOSE SOME STYLE.** Each try to find a balance, compromise, or split-the-difference between the two views, needs, and goals. Both Win something- Both lose something orientation. **Disadvantages:** It's pretty simplistic, with simplistic solutions that don't take into account a full understanding of the problem. **Advantages:** It's relatively quick and dirty; the give-and-take allows some negotiation.

Based on the Kenneth Thomas & Ralph Kilmann conflict model, 1972

COUPLES' PROBLEM AND CONFLICT INVENTORY

All couples have conflicts, disagreements, and difficulties. This is a natural part of all close relationships. However, in order to ultimately solve problems, you first need to identify them, and to identify how serious or important each is. Some areas in which other couples have identified problems include: the division of responsibility, money, sex, managing children, making decisions, spending time and activities together, alcohol and drugs, parents-relatives-ex-partners, friends, jealousy, communication, anger and abusiveness, trust, affection, commitment, independence, unrealistic expectations, career decisions, work, and religion.

This worksheet will help you identify relationship conflicts and problems by following three steps. First, identify MILD IRRITATIONS OR PET PEEVES. Second, identify MORE SERIOUS AND SIGNIFICANT ISSUES. Third, remember that even though you may have conflicts and problems, there are still THINGS WHICH ARE POSITIVE IN YOUR RELATIONSHIP and things which you like and appreciate about your partner.

THE MILD IRRITATIONS, PET PEEVES, OR THINGS I WANT TO KNOW MORE ABOUT IN MY RELATIONSHIP ARE:

List the Problems, Conflicts, Difficulties, or Disagreements.

1. _____

2. _____

3. _____

4. _____

THE MORE SERIOUS AND SIGNIFICANT ISSUES IN MY RELATIONSHIP ARE:

List the Problems, Conflicts, Difficulties, or Disagreements.

1. _____

2. _____

3. _____

4. _____

THE THINGS WHICH I APPRECIATE OR LIKE ABOUT MY PARTNER OR MY RELATIONSHIP ARE:

List the traits, qualities, characteristics, attitudes, behaviors, activities, etc.

1. _____
2. _____
3. _____
4. _____
5. _____
6. _____

© Clyde M. Feldman, 1993

TIME OUT SKILLS

Below are skills which other people have developed to successfully AVOID VIOLENCE AND ABUSE by *taking action early*.

RECOGNIZE YOUR "EARLY WARNING SIGNS" OF UPSET

1. Our signs of muscle tension, stomach upset, cursing, yelling, threatening, or following from room to room alert us that the anger cycle is beginning to snow-ball. It may end in a blow-up if we ignore these signals and wait and see what happens.

2. Know where you are at on your own personal anger "thermometer".

   ```
   0 - - - - - - - - - - - - - - - - - - - - - 100
   NO ANGER                        EXPLOSIVE WITH ANGER
   ```

3. Know what kind of upset feelings you have that make you most angry. Frustrated, insulted, hurt, insecure, jealous, revengeful are feelings we all have and we can learn to take care of ourselves without using violence and aggression.

4. Recognize when the argument has gone on too long and can only end in disaster.

5. Tell your partner about your plan to interrupt a blow-up by leaving that place for some period of time. Make sure they know that YOU DO PLAN TO COME BACK and ROUGHLY HOW LONG YOU PLAN TO BE GONE.

DURING THE TIME-OUT SEPARATION PERIOD

1. Remember any rules you and your partner have made about WHERE *NOT* TO GO, WHAT *NOT* TO DO, and WHO *NOT* TO SEE.

2. *DON'T DRINK* as a way to avoid facing up to your problems.

3. Do something that is "physical" and not harmful to yourself or others like taking a walk, playing ball, jogging, yardwork....

4. Take a deep breath, hold it as long as you can, and let it out slowly. Repeat this as often as you need it.

5. Consciously relax tight places in your body like your jaws, neck, shoulders, and fists.

6. Get involved in a more neutral and positive activity like watching T.V., going to the store, listening to music, contacting a friend or family member who understands you.

7. *Practice "cool" thinking.* Remember to see a picture of how you want the situation to turn out.

8. Rehearse what statements, feelings, or requests you want to share with the other person ahead of time. Practice mentally before you return to "time-in".

DURING TIME-IN

1. If you don't come back in a reasonable amount of time and with a more neutral attitude, leaving can end up being <u>AN AVOIDANCE TACTIC</u> or just another way of <u>GETTING BACK AT SOMEONE</u>.

2. Make an agreement with your partner to set up a time and place to talk where:

    - Both people feel comfortable and not frightened.
    - There are no distractions like T.V., kids, or other company.
    - Each persons gets some time to talk without being interrupted.

3. Use *Good Communication* techniques, NOT DIRTY FIGHTING TECHNIQUES:

    <u>Sit down</u> rather than standing up while you talk. Ask the other person to sit down too.

    <u>Be a listener</u> by facing each other, taking turns talking and listening, and letting them know, in your own words, that you understand what they are saying.

    <u>Handle criticism</u> by not taking it so personally and by finding some way to agree with some point they are making.

    <u>Accept their opinion</u> as different than yours rather than it being "wrong", "stupid", or "crazy".

    <u>Express your feelings</u> in words instead of holding them in, letting them build up, and showing them through force.

    <u>Make requests not demands</u> by asking them to do more of the positive things that will help you and the relationship.

Give appreciations and compliments by telling them at least ONE thing they have done recently that you like. Break the cycle of hearing only criticism and dissatisfaction.

© Clyde M. Feldman, 1995

Clyde M. Feldman, Ph.D.

"TIME-OUT" CONTRACT

STEP 1: ### IDENTIFYING EARLY WARNING SIGNS

The first step in taking a TIME-OUT is knowing when to take it. Early warning signs give us a clue that our body, thoughts, and feelings are changing. These warning signs tell us to call a TIME-OUT.

LIST YOUR EARLY WARNING SIGNS OR THOSE OF THE OTHER PERSON.

_____

_____

_____

ON AN ANGER AND UPSET SCALE FROM 1 TO 100
(1=extremely calm; 100=extremely angry/upset)

AT WHAT NUMBER WOULD YOU PROBABLY WANT TO CALL YOUR TIME OUT?

_____

STEP 2: ### SIGNAL FOR A TIME-OUT

Once you identify your warning signs, it is important to signal for a time-out. The signal could be a sign, a phrase, or a statement. But it must be neutral and nonthreatening.

MY TIME-OUT SIGNAL IS: _____

STEP 3: ### PHYSICALLY SEPARATING

Once TIME-OUT has been signaled and acknowledged by the other person, those involved should physically separate for some period of time. Decide on a neutral and safe place where you will go and how long the TIME-OUT will probably last. Both parties need to know this information in advance so the act of separating does not add fuel to the fire and become an additional conflict.

MY NEUTRAL AND SAFE PLACE(S) TO GO DURING THE TIME-OUT ARE: _____

_____

THE LENGTH OF MY TIME-OUT WILL USUALLY BE: _____

_____

PLACES <u>NOT</u> TO GO AND THINGS <u>NOT</u> TO DO: _____

_____

MY CONCERNS OR WORRIES ABOUT THE TIME-OUT ARE: _____

_____

STEP 4: *COOLING-DOWN AND CONTROLLING ANGER*

During TIME-OUT it is essential that anger control techniques be used in order to prevent any blow-ups. If not, you can become even more angry and upset during the separation period. Some key techniques are: (a) blowing off some steam by doing something physical like walking, biking, or playing ball, (b) relaxing by deep breathing, relaxing tight muscles, or music, (c) talking things out with someone who knows and understands you, (d) using cool-thoughts, picturing how you want this situation to turn out, analyzing your part in the problem, and (e) practicing what you want to say when you come back together.

THE COOLING-DOWN AND ANGER CONTROL TECHNIQUES I WILL USE TO CHANGE THE WAY I'M THINKING, FEELING, AND ACTING ARE:

_____

_____

_____

_____

STEP 5: *TIME-IN*

Once you have cooled down during the separation period, you must return to TIME-IN. That means coming back together and either having a discussion about the problem OR negotiating a time and place for having the discussion sometime soon. Only focus on one issue at a time. If you find yourself getting upset or see that the discussion is escalating into verbal or physical abuse, do not hesitate to call another TIME-OUT.

THE MOST IMPORTANT THINGS I NEED TO BE ABLE TO DO AND SAY DURING TIME-IN ARE:

_____

_____

_____

I AGREE TO RESPECT THIS TIME-OUT CONTRACT.

SIGNED BY: _____ **DATE:** _____

SIGNED BY: _____ **DATE:** _____

© Clyde M. Feldman, 1995

FOUR-STEP PROBLEM-SOLVING PROCEDURE

THE GROUND RULES

1. <u>Make A Specific Time</u> to sit down and discuss a problem ahead of time.
2. <u>Set A Time And Place</u> that's comfortable for both people, with few distractions.
3. <u>Focus On One Issue</u> and stick to that issue.
4. <u>Only Bring Up Things That Are Related To The Problem</u> and solving the problem.
5. <u>Stay Focused On Problems That You Are Experiencing Now</u>. No gripes from the past.
6. <u>Take A WIN-WIN Attitude</u>. This means that you are ready to collaborate and compromise so that the decisions you make together will have something good for BOTH PEOPLE.
7. <u>Take Turns Talking And Listening</u>. One person speaks while the other listens. Then change roles.

☞ **THE LISTENER SHOULD:**
- Show with your body language and voice tone that you are really involved and really want to listen.
- Listen carefully even when you don't agree.
- Ask "open" questions if you're unclear, confused, or need more information.
- Check out your assumptions... they may be WRONG.
- Try not to be defensive or counterattack.
- Put yourself in the other person's place.
- Summarize in your own words what you heard them say.

☞ **THE SPEAKER SHOULD:**
- Put your thoughts and feelings into WORDS.
- Don't bring up the past. Stay focused on the HERE and NOW.
- Talk about YOUR feelings, YOUR thoughts, and YOUR actions, not just what the other person does.

THE PROBLEM-SOLVING STEPS

STEP 1: **DEFINE AND UNDERSTAND THE PROBLEM**

    A. Each person describe the problem from their own point of view, talking about their own thoughts and feelings.

    B. Each person give a few specific, real life, examples of the problem.

    C. Each person talk about how the problem affects them. Why is it a problem for you?

    D. Each person take responsibility for some part in the problem, no matter how small, and describe what they do or don't do that keeps it a problem.

STEP 2: **UNDERSTAND WHAT THINGS WOULD BE LIKE IF THE PROBLEM WERE SOLVED**

    A. Each person imagine that after you both go to sleep tonight a "magical" event or "miracle" happens, and the problem is completely solved. Since you were sleeping, you didn't know that it happened. What do you notice the next day that indicates that the problem has been solved?

    B. Each person describe how things would be better (emotionally, psychologically, behaviorally) if the problem didn't exist anymore?

    C. Each person try to think of a time when the problem was either not present or was better (e.g., less intense or less frequent). When was that? What was happening then? What was each person doing to help make these "EXCEPTIONS" happen?

    D. Each person list your wants and needs. State the things you would like MORE OF from the other person, the relationship, or from others in your life.

STEP 3: **BRAINSTORM POSSIBLE SOLUTIONS AND MAKE A MUTUAL AGREEMENT TO PUT ONE PLAN INTO ACTION ON A TRIAL BASIS**

    A. Each person generate a list of at least 3 possible plans for solving the problem - things that you think, guess, hope could be done differently to improve the problem. Be creative, humorous, and daring. Don't worry if an idea on your list seems crazy or impractical.

B. As a pair, go though each of the possible solutions and rank their good and bad points. Ask yourself:

- Will it help reach our goal and improve this problem or even solve it?
- Do we have the time and money it would take to do it?
- Do I feel comfortable about it and motivated enough about it?

C. As a pair, pick one best alternative solution to try out for a trial period of time. BE WILLING TO COMPROMISE in order to decide on one trial plan.

D. As a pair, make a clear agreement that states what will be done, who will do what, when it will be done, how often it will be done, and how long you will try out the plan before you stop and decide if it is working.

STEP 4: **EVALUATE HOW THE PLAN IS WORKING**

Did each of us do what we agreed to do?   If No, What went wrong?
If Yes, Is the problem better than before?

If the Problem's Better, What's going better? How can we keep this plan going?

If the Problem's *Not* Better , What is still not working? Should we modify this plan, or try out another alternative solution on our list?

© Clyde M. Feldman, 1995

Clyde M. Feldman, Ph.D.

WORKSHEET FOR MUTUAL PROBLEM SOLVING

STEP 1:

The Thoughts And Feelings Of _____ About Why This is A Problem Are:

The Thoughts And Feelings Of _____ About Why This Is A Problem Are:

The Way _____ Contributes To The Problem is:

The Way _____ Contributes To The Problem Is:

STEP 2:

What would be happening differently after the "miracle" according to _____ is:

What would be happening differently after the "miricle" according to _____ is:

The list of needs and wants of _____ is:

    a.

    b.

    c.

    d.

The list of needs and wants of _____ is:

    a.

    b.

    c.

    d,

STEP 3:

Solutions Suggested By _____ include:

    a.

    b.

    c.

The Solutions Suggested By _____ include:

   a.

   b.

   c.

Our Agreed Upon Trial Plan For The Next _____ is: (Who does what, how often, when)

STEP 4:

At The End Of The Trial Period, Answer The Questions Below:

   What Went Well?

   What Didn't Go So Well?

   What Could We Do To Improve The Plan To Make it Work Better?

© Clyde M. Feldman, 1994

NEGATIVE REACTION WORKSHEET FOR CONFLICT

SITUATION: Describe the situation. It may be one where you were by yourself or with others.

___

___

___

NEGATIVE FEELINGS: List as many as you had in the situation (angry, rejected, hurt, frustrated) and also rate the intensity from 1 (low) to 10 (high)

___

___

___

AUTOMATIC THOUGHTS: Write down the negative thoughts, beliefs, assumptions, expectations, and mental pictures that were going through your mind about yourself, other people, the situation, the future, etc. Also rate your belief in each of these from 1% (not really) to 100% (completely)

___

___

___

___

OUTCOME: What did you say or do that was negative, was an over-reaction, or escalated the situation.

___

___

© Clyde M. Feldman, 1994

FOUR WAYS TO HELP CREATE POSITIVE SELF-TALK AND POSITIVE MENTAL PICTURES

YOUR POSITIVE PAST EXPERIENCE

Remember, think of, or find a time in the past, in a similar kind of situation, when you were able to handle things more like you want to now. Remember that now and put yourself back into that situation. What were you able to say to yourself, believe, remind yourself, picture to yourself, feel emotionally, and do back then that would help you in the current situation?

FUTURE PROJECTION

Imagine that you could project yourself into the future (__ months / years from now), at a point in time when you have already figured out how to handle this kind of situation. What are you able to say to yourself, believe, remind yourself, picture to yourself, feel emotionally, and do in the future that would help you in the present?

A COACH OR MODEL

Think about someone - real or fictional, public or you know personally, living or passed away - who knows how to handle this kind of situation the way you wish you could. What would they coach you to say to yourself, believe, remind yourself, picture to yourself, feel emotionally, and do in the current situation? What would they be able to do say to themselves, picture, or do that you could try out for yourself?

A MAGIC WAND

Imagine you had a magic wand and you could use it on yourself to handle this kind of situation they way you wish you could. What would it give you the ability to say to yourself, believe, remind yourself, picture to yourself, feel emotionally, and do in this situation?

© Adapted from NLP and Solution-focused models by Clyde M. Feldman, 2010

POSITIVE COUNTER-STATEMENTS AND PICTURES WORKSHEET FOR REDUCING CONFLICT

WRITE DOWN YOUR NEGATIVE THOUGHTS, BELIEFS, ASSUMPTIONS, EXPECTATIONS, AND MENTAL PICTURES DURING CONFLICT:

1A. _____

2A. _____

3A. _____

4A. _____

CREATE A POSITIVE COUNTER-STATEMENT, POSITIVE COPING STATEMENT, OR POSITIVE MENTAL PICTURE FOR EACH OF THE ABOVE:

1B. _____

2B. _____

3B. _____

4B. _____

SECTION 3:

ANGER AND DOMESTIC VIOLENCE TOOLS

Clyde M. Feldman, Ph.D.

ANGER INVENTORY

NAME: _____   DATE: _____

Everybody gets angry from time to time. A number of statements that people have used to describe the times that they get angry are included below. Please circle a number from 1 to 7 that means how strongly you agree with the statements below.

1	2	3	4	5	6	7
Strongly **DIS**agree						Strongly Agree

1. I tend to get angry more often than most people do.   1 2 3 4 5 6 7

2. Other people seem to stay calmer than me in similar circumstances.   1 2 3 4 5 6 7

3. I harbor grudges that I don't tell anyone about.   1 2 3 4 5 6 7

4. I try to get even when I'm angry with someone.   1 2 3 4 5 6 7

5. I'm secretly quite critical of others.   1 2 3 4 5 6 7

6. It's pretty easy to make me angry.   1 2 3 4 5 6 7

7. I don't get myself angry, people make me angry.   1 2 3 4 5 6 7

8. I've met many people who are supposed to be experts who are no better than I.   1 2 3 4 5 6 7

9. Something makes me angry almost every day.   1 2 3 4 5 6 7

10. I often feel angrier than I think I should.   1 2 3 4 5 6 7

11. I feel guilty about expressing my anger.   1 2 3 4 5 6 7

12. When I'm angry, I take it out on whoever is around.   1 2 3 4 5 6 7

13. Even my friends have habits that annoy and bother me a lot.   1 2 3 4 5 6 7

14. I'm surprised at how often I feel angry.   1 2 3 4 5 6 7

15. Even after I tell someone that I'm angry with them, I have a hard time forgetting about it and putting it out of my mine. 1 2 3 4 5 6 7

16. I feel like people talk about me behind my back. 1 2 3 4 5 6 7

17. At times, I feel angry for no specific reason. 1 2 3 4 5 6 7

18. I can get myself pretty angry just by thinking about something that happened in the past. 1 2 3 4 5 6 7

19. Once somebody pushes my buttons, they can't hold me responsible for what happens afterwards. 1 2 3 4 5 6 7

20. Even when I don't show somebody how angry I am, it stays on my mind for a long time. 1 2 3 4 5 6 7

21. People can bother me just by being around. 1 2 3 4 5 6 7

22. When I get angry, I stay angry for hours. 1 2 3 4 5 6 7

23. I have a bad temper. 1 2 3 4 5 6 7

24. I try to talk to people without letting them know that I'm angry. 1 2 3 4 5 6 7

25. When I get angry, I don't calm down as fast as most people. 1 2 3 4 5 6 7

26. I get so angry, I feel like a might lose control. 1 2 3 4 5 6 7

27. If I let people see the way I really feel, I'd be considered a hard person to get along with. 1 2 3 4 5 6 7

28. I am on my guard with people who are friendlier than I expect. 1 2 3 4 5 6 7

29. It's difficult for me to let other people know that I'm angry. 1 2 3 4 5 6 7

30-40. I get VERY angry when:

   Someone I know makes me feel like they let me down. 1 2 3 4 5 6 7

   Someone I know makes me feel ignored. 1 2 3 4 5 6 7

Something blocks my plans.		1 2 3 4 5 6 7
Someone I know doesn't take my advice.		1 2 3 4 5 6 7
Someone I know makes me feel embarrassed.		1 2 3 4 5 6 7
I have to take orders from someone less capable than I.		1 2 3 4 5 6 7
I have to work with incompetent people.		1 2 3 4 5 6 7
I do something stupid.		1 2 3 4 5 6 7
I'm not given credit for something I have done.		1 2 3 4 5 6 7
Someone I know disagrees with me on how to do something.		1 2 3 4 5 6 7
Someone I know says negative things about me to others.		1 2 3 4 5 6 7

41. I keep myself from being too angry so I don't end up losing control.   1 2 3 4 5 6 7

42. I'm a hot-headed person.   1 2 3 4 5 6 7

43. I have a fiery temper when provoked.   1 2 3 4 5 6 7

44. When I'm right I've got to prove it.   1 2 3 4 5 6 7

45. When I'm really angry at someone, they have to stay and hear it, not walk away.   1 2 3 4 5 6 7

46. When talking doesn't work, a show of power can often get the point across.   1 2 3 4 5 6 7

47. I never back down from a challenge.   1 2 3 4 5 6 7

48. When people disagree with me, they're trying to disrespect me.   1 2 3 4 5 6 7

49. The best rule to use in arguments is "an eye for an eye, a tooth for a tooth".   1 2 3 4 5 6 7

50. People that know me would say I have a bad temper.   1 2 3 4 5 6 7

SCORING

ADD UP YOUR SCORES FOR ALL 50 QUESTIONS= _____.

IF YOUR SCORE IS 1-90, YOU PROBABLY <u>DON'T</u> HAVE SIGNIFICANT ANGER ISSUES.

IF YOUR SCORE IS 91-175, YOU MAY HAVE SOME <u>MINOR</u> ANGER ISSUES.

IF YOUR SCORE IS 176-265, YOU MAY HAVE SOME <u>SIGNIFICANT</u> ANGER ISSUES.

IF YOUR SCORE IS 266-350, YOU MAY HAVE SOME <u>VERY SIGNIFICANT</u> ANGER ISSUES.

Judith Siegel, 1986

Clyde M. Feldman, Ph.D.

DOMESTIC VIOLENCE RISK ASSESSMENT INVENTORY

NAME: _____   DATE: _____

PART ONE

PLEASE CIRCLE THE ANSWER THAT FITS FOR YOU

1. My use of alcohol or drugs can be a problem for me or for others around me.

    NEVER   RARELY   SOMETIMES   OFTEN

2. When I was growing up, I saw my parents, step-parents, relatives get verbally or physically abusive <u>with each other</u>.

    NEVER   RARELY   SOMETIMES   OFTEN

3. When I was growing up, my parents, step-parents, older brothers/sister, or relatives were verbally or physically abusive <u>to me.</u>

    NEVER   RARELY   SOMETIMES   OFTEN

4. In my current relationship (wife, girlfriend, boyfriend, etc.) my partner tries to provoke a fight or tries to keep me from leaving.

    NEVER   RARELY   SOMETIMES   OFTEN

5. Besides my partner, I talk to one or more close friends about problems in my life.

    NEVER   RARELY   SOMETIMES   OFTEN

6. In my current relationship (wife, girlfriend, boyfriend, etc.) we argue and disagree.

    NEVER   RARELY   SOMETIMES   OFTEN

7. These days, my satisfaction with my current relationship is . . .

    VERY LOW   LOW   MEDIUM   HIGH

8. These days, my stress level is . . .

    VERY LOW   LOW   MEDIUM   HIGH

9. The statement: "I don't get myself angry, people make me angry" is . . .

    NOT TRUE   SOMETIMES TRUE   OFTEN TRUE   ALWAYS TRUE

10. My temper is . . .

    VERY GOOD   SOMEWHAT GOOD   SOMEWHAT BAD   VERY BAD

PART TWO:

HERE IS A LIST OF BEHAVIORS THAT MANY MEN AND WOMEN SAID HAVE BEEN USED BY THEIR CURRENT PARTNERS, FORMER PARTNERS, OR FAMILY MEMBERS.

PLEASE CIRCLE ABOUT HOW OFTEN <u>YOU HAVE USED</u> THESE BEHAVIORS DURING THE <u>LAST SIX MONTHS</u> TOWARD A PARTNER OR FORMER PARTNER (WIFE, GIRLFRIEND, BOYFRIEND, ETC.) OR TOWARDS A FAMILY MEMBER (PARENT, BROTHER, SISTER).

1. Called them names, swore at them, said insulting, ridiculing, intimidating, or degrading things to them.

    ZERO   1 TIME   2 OR MORE TIMES

2. Verbally threatened to do something to them that they would not like or said things to scare them.

    ZERO   1 TIME   2 OR MORE TIMES

3. Pushed, grabbed, shoved, or held them down.

    ZERO   1 TIME   2 OR MORE TIMES

4. Scratched them, bit them, spit at them, pulled their hair, etc.

    ZERO   1 TIME   2 OR MORE TIMES

5. Broke or damaged something (like punched or kicked a wall or door, ripped something up, broke a window or a household object).

    ZERO   1 TIME   2 OR MORE TIMES

6. Threw something (not necessarily at them).

    ZERO   1 TIME   2 OR MORE TIMES

7. Slapped, hit, or kicked them.

    ZERO   1 TIME   2 OR MORE TIMES

8. Made them do something humiliating or degrading.

    ZERO   1 TIME   2 OR MORE TIMES

9. Followed them or checked up on them (like listened to their phone calls, checked their mileage, called them repeatedly at work).

    ZERO   1 TIME   2 OR MORE TIMES

10. Pressured them to do something sexual or to have sex.

    ZERO   1 TIME   2 OR MORE TIMES

11. Threatened them with or used a knife, a gun, or any object that might be used as a weapon.

    ZERO   1 TIME   2 OR MORE TIMES

12. **Punched them.**

> ZERO   1 TIME   2 OR MORE TIMES

13. **Physically stopped them, or tried to stop them, from doing something they wanted to do or going somewhere they wanted to go.**

> ZERO   1 TIME   2 OR MORE TIMES

14. **Tried to choke or strangle them.**

> ZERO   1 TIME   2 OR MORE TIMES

Scoring Instructions

Part One: items 1-10 (30 points total)

1. FOR ITEMS #1, 2, 3, 4, 6, 8, 9, 10 COUNT:

   NEVER/ VERY LOW/ NOT TRUE/ VERY GOOD= 0
   RARELY/ LOW/ SOMETIMES TRUE/ SOMEWHAT GOOD= 1
   SOMETIMES/ MEDIUM/ OFTEN TRUE/ SOMEWHAT BAD= 2
   OFTEN/ HIGH/ ALWAYS TRUE/ VERY BAD= 3

2. FOR ITEMS # 5, 7 COUNT:

   NEVER/ VERY LOW= 3
   RARELY/ LOW= 2
   SOMETIMES/ MEDIUM= 1
   OFTEN/ HIGH= 0

PART TWO: ITEMS 1-15 (70 POINTS TOTAL)

1. FOR ITEMS #1, 2, 4, 6, 8, 9, 10 COUNT:

   ZERO= 0   1 TIME= 2   2 OR MORE TIMES= 4

2. FOR ITEMS #3, 5, 7, 11, 12, 13, 14 COUNT:

   ZERO= 0   1 TIME= 3   2 OR MORE TIMES= 6

INTERPRETATION OF THE SCORES

ADD UP THE TOTAL SCORE. INTERPRETATION SHOULD BE BASED UPON YOUR PROFESSIONAL JUDGEMENT AND KNOWLEDGE OF CLIENT'S CIRCUMSTANCES, CLINICAL PROBLEMS, AND ISSUES. A GENERAL GUIDELINE I HAVE USED IS:

    LOW RISK   = 0-15
    MODERATE RISK   = 16-32
    HIGH RISK   = 33-49
    VERY HIGH RISK   = 50-100

© Clyde M. Feldman, 2000

ATTITUDE CHECKLIST FOR ANGER AND VIOLENCE

Please write in a number, FROM 0% (NOT TRUE) TO 100% (COMPLETELY TRUE), in each of the boxes below meaning "how much do I believe this statement is true for me".

ATTITUDES WHICH MAY KEEP ME FROM RECOGNIZING MY PART IN THE PROBLEM

I'm the one who's been most hurt and abused. [_____]

I'm not the one to blame for the fights in my relationship. [_____]

If I have acted aggressively or abusively, it's only because I was drinking. [_____]

I've never really hurt anyone. [_____]

I don't get myself angry, people make me angry. [_____]

If you start the fight, I can't be held responsible for what I do afterwards. [_____]

I always take the blame. [_____]

Once somebody pushes my buttons, the situation is out of my control. [_____]

I'm not the one who needs to change in order for the problems to get solved. [_____]

THE BEST ATTITUDE I CAN TAKE ABOUT MY OWN RESPONSIBILITY IN PROBLEMS IS:

ATTITUDES WHICH MAY KEEP ME FROM COMMUNICATING & PROBLEM-SOLVING

If I've gotten physical, the other person deserved it. [_____]

If someone verbally attacks me, cheats me, or lies to me I have a right to get physical. [_____]

When I'm right I've got to prove it. [_____]

Talking about things only makes them worse. [_____]

Nobody hurts me and walks away without getting the worst of it. [_____]

Some things will only change when you use threats. [_____]

Things have got to be my way. [_____]

When I'm pissed at someone, they have to stay and hear it, not walk away. [_____]

When talking doesn't work, a show of power usually gets the point across. [_____]

I never back down from a challenge. [_____]

Getting physical gets the argument over quickly, instead of dragging it out. [_____]

When people disagree with me, they're trying to disrespect me. [_____]

The best rule to use in arguments is "an eye for an eye, a tooth for a tooth". [_____]

THE BEST ATTITUDE I CAN TAKE ABOUT MY OWN USE OF POWER AND FORCE IS:

ATTITUDES WHICH MAY KEEP ME FEELING BAD ABOUT MYSELF AND FEELING DEFENSIVE

There's no one I can talk to about my problems. [_____]

I'm not living up to my own expectations. [_____]

I'm not capable of changing the way I handle angry situations. [_____]

I believe in keeping my feelings to myself. [_____]

I need a lot of reminders and reassurance that my partner is faithful and true. [_____]

If I back down from a challenge, I'll lose my pride. [_____]

I should be able to solve my problems without asking for help. [_____]

I don't trust most people. [_____]

Expressing my feelings will only make me look stupid or humiliate me. [_____]

I won't be the one that ends this relationship, no matter how bad it gets. [_____]

Inside, I believe that I'm not really good enough or adequate enough. [_____]

THE BEST ATTITUDE I CAN TAKE ABOUT MY OWN SELF-IMAGE AND SELF-WORTH IS:

ATTITUDES WHICH MAY KEEP ME FROM TREATING A PARTNER AS VALUABLE AND EQUAL

I expect a partner to know how I feel without me having to say it. [_____]

A partner shouldn't have the right to withhold sex from me. [_____]

As head of the household, I should have the final say about decisions. [_____]

I shouldn't have to let a partner know where I'm going or what I'm doing. [_____]

Most partners are not capable of changing. [_____]

A partner shouldn't have the right to spend time wherever and with whomever they wants. [_____]

I need to have control over where a partner is, who they're with, and what they're doing for the relationship to work. [_____]

A lot of the time you have to lie to a partner and tell them what they wants to hear in order to get what you want from them. [_____]

Once a partner has cheated on you, cheating on them is fair play. [_____]

Women and men are supposed to have very different roles in relationships, so you shouldn't try to reverse them or try to mix them up. [_____]

Even romantic partners are out to mess with your mind. [_____]

THE BEST ATTITUDE I CAN TAKE ABOUT MY CLOSE RELATIONSHIPS WITH PARTNERS IS:

© Clyde M. Feldman, 1995

Clyde M. Feldman, Ph.D.

FIVE TYPES OF DOMESTIC ABUSE CHECKLIST

PHYSICAL ABUSE

- [ ] Blocking the person, trapping them in a room, holding them down, or restraining them.
- [ ] Breaking or damaging things like furniture, clothes, equipment, the phone, or the car.
- [ ] Throwing things across the room, at doors or walls, or at the other person.
- [ ] Punching, hitting, kicking, or damaging walls, doors, or windows.
- [ ] Hitting, slapping, pushing, kicking, shaking, pulling hair, scratching, biting, or punching.
- [ ] Choking, stabbing, or threatening the person with a weapon.

PSYCHOLOGICAL, EMOTIONAL, AND VERBAL ABUSE

- [ ] Making intimidating looks, gestures, and threats.
- [ ] Verbal attacks, put downs, name calling, humiliating comments, character assassination.
- [ ] Making threats to do something to hurt the other person or to hurt yourself (suicide).
- [ ] Saying that the other person caused everything, denying that any abuse happened.
- [ ] Controlling what the other person does, who they see and talk to, or where they go by stranding them, limiting their contact outside the house, controlling their telephone calls, checking-up on them, or setting time limits on what they do.
- [ ] Playing mind games by telling them they are going crazy, pretending nothing happened, or hiding things.
- [ ] Abusing pets.
- [ ] Threatening to do something to the children as a way of getting back at the other person.

- ☐ Threatening to take the children away or trying to keep the other person from seeing or being with the children as punishment.
- ☐ Taking anger and frustration about the other person out on the children.
- ☐ Repeated criticizing and putting down of the other person as a parent.
- ☐ Punishing or being purposely cruel to the children as a way of indirectly hurting or punishing the other person.
- ☐ Acting like a "dictator" by treating others like servants, deciding all rules and decisions.

SEXUAL ABUSE

- ☐ Pressuring them, forcing them, or threatening them into unwanted sexual acts.
- ☐ Calling them demeaning sexual names like "bitch", "whore", "slut", "frigid".
- ☐ Sexually fondling, grabbing, or groping them in public or at home when unwanted.
- ☐ Being unfaithful by having affairs or bringing home sexually transmitted diseases.
- ☐ Constantly accusing them of unfaithfulness, interrogating them, or checking up on them.

ECONOMIC ABUSE

- ☐ Not letting a partner have access to family income
- ☐ Putting them on an allowance, making then ask for money, or forcing them to turn over their paycheck.
- ☐ Stopping a partner from getting or keeping a job.
- ☐ Keeping a partner from having any say or role in deciding how money is spent.
- ☐ Spending money needed for utilities, rent, food on things like drugs, alcohol, or gambling.

NEGLECT OF CHILDREN (active or passive)

- ☐ Isolating children from others, or leaving them by themselves for long periods of time.
- ☐ Not providing or withholding necessary food, shelter, clothes, medical attention, or personal care from children.
- ☐ Using physical restraints on children or locking them in a room or closet.
- ☐ Using excessive medication to manage or sedate children.

© Clyde M. Feldman, 2000

EARLY WARNING SIGNS IN ANGRY SITUATIONS

Many times, it's difficult to look back on an angry or aggressive incident and remember anything except the final "blow-up". The "blow-up" may happen after only a few minutes, or it may happen after hours of building up angry and upset feelings. People have described themselves during a "blow-up" as being "out of control", "on automatic", "on impulse", and "crazy". They are describing a time when things happen fast, when they feel overwhelmed, and when they often do and say things that don't seem like them.

The reason why angry situations seem this way is because we have turned on a kind of "AUTOMATIC PILOT" when our normal controls get overloaded. This AUTOMATIC PILOT is guided by THREE TYPES OF RAPID-FIRE MESSAGES:

MESSAGE #1: PHYSICAL BODY WARNING SIGNS

Almost always, certain things happen to our bodies as we get more angry and upset. Adrenaline starts to pump and our heart rate speeds up, our muscles get tighter, our face feels flushed, and our hands may start to shake or sweat. Some body warning signs are easier to see and hear like when we can get loud fast, stare someone down, get right in someone's face, or follow them from room to room. All of these things are physical body reactions when we feel provoked, pissed-off, or defensive. These are the earliest warning signs that our automatic pilot may be taking over. Our bodies actually begin to physically prepare for a fight.

MESSAGE #2: NEGATIVE FEELINGS

Probably the most common emotional feeling we have in upset and aggressive situations is *ANGER*. If we were feeling good most of the day, those feelings can change rapidly. And chances are we'll rapidly change the way we've been acting too. This *ANGER MESSAGE* signals our strong dislike about something someone did or said. Often this is someone we know well and so our "buttons" get pushed more easily.

But our automatic pilot usually COVERS UP OR EVEN IGNORES a range of other feelings we have about the situation, the other person, and about ourselves. Behind the anger, people have felt hurt, put down, frustrated, insecure, discouraged, unappreciated, or guilty, for example. But when the automatic pilot takes over, these feelings often get tuned out and turned into anger. How we handle these situations depends on knowing ALL the emotions we are feeling, not just the anger. Here is a fuller list of negative feelings we may be having, in addition to anger.

Unimportant	Insecure	Strong-headed	Overwhelmed	Betrayed
Foolish	Worthless	Humiliated	Put-down	Jealous
Criticized	Controlled	Unaccepted	Awkward	Concerned
Quiet	Scared	Guilty	Outranged	Depressed
Disgusted	Needy	Inferior	Suspicious	Uncertain
Weary	Desperate	Uneasy	Doubting	Rejected
Anxious	Nervous	Worried	Hurt	Deprived
Insulted	Possessive	Inhibited	Remorseful	Uptight
Unsympathetic	Confused	Disappointed	Afraid	Resentful
Ignored	Insincere	Withdrawn	Shut-down	Hateful
Sad	Helpless	Belittled	Defensive	Used
Dominated	Terrified	Impatient	Domineering	Insecure
Tired	Preoccupied	Timid	Frustrated	Macho
Curious	Irritable	Aggravated	Manipulated	Tense
Disillusioned	Inadequate	Threatened	Useless	Pressured
Sorry	Discouraged	Uncomfortable	Defeated	Unsure
Embarrassed	Belligerent	Hopeless	Incompetent	Justified
Persecuted	Protective	Guarded	Stubborn	Touchy
Victimized	Dependent	Envious	Ungrateful	Dejected
Misunderstood	Stupid	Indecisive	Offended	Proud
Lonely	Pessimistic	Unappreciated	Revengeful	Superior
Unsuccessful	Ineffective	Distrustful	Trapped	Powerless

MESSAGE #3: HOT THINKING

The central control system that guides our automatic pilot is our thinking - the HOT thoughts, the HOT pictures, the HOT instructions, and the HOT attitudes that go through our heads in angry and aggressive situations. This thinking may happen in just a few minutes or even seconds. Although we don't realize it, we tell ourselves to tense up, to take a defensive attitude, and to take aggressive and angry action.

As the physical body warning signs and angry feelings begin to mount, others have had these HOT THOUGHT and PICTURES:

- "I HAVE TO SHUT HER UP ANY WAY I CAN!"
- "I KNOW HE DOES THIS JUST TO MESS WITH MY MIND!"
- "NOBODY SAYS THAT TO ME AND GETS AWAY WITH IT!"
- "I DON'T GIVE A SHIT IF YOU LEAVE ME!"
- "MEN ARE OUT TO SCREW YOU OVER!"
- "WHEN I SEE HIM LOOKING AT ANOTHER WOMAN, I WANNA GET REVENGE!"
- "IF SHE HITS ME, I DEFINITELY WILL HIT BACK - AND HARD!"
- "WHEN SHE DRESSES LIKE THAT, SHE DESERVES TO BE TAUGHT A LESSON!

HOT THINKING sometimes has to do with taking things *too personally* when there is no need to. When we take things others say and do too personally, we OVER-REACT. We can get distracted from what is really important by trying to get even instead of finding a solution to the problem. We can also get baited into the same argument over and over again.

HOT THINKING sometimes has to do with feeling like things are out of control and so we think that we need to *take control*. We may take control of the situation for five minutes, but never take time to think it through long enough to make it turn out the way we really wanted it to.

HOT THINKING sometimes has to do with thinking that we may *not be good enough*, doubting ourselves, being unsure and insecure. As a result, we may never let ourselves relax, believe in ourselves, and try out new and better ways of handling disagreements and conflict.

© Clyde M. Feldman and David Harvey, 1992

EARLY WARNING SIGNS WORKSHEET

THE KINDS OF SITUATIONS OR THINGS THAT PEOPLE DO THAT PUSH MY BUTTONS, TICK ME OFF, BUG ME, GET TO ME, OR I CAN'T STAND ARE: (examples: people doing stupid things when they know better, people not doing their job, people trying to control me, people getting in my face, people that won't back down, people talking back to me, lazy people, people cutting me off in traffic, people asking me something I don't have an answer to, etc.)

(1) _____

(2) _____

(3) _____

(4) _____

TWO RECENT SITUATIONS WHERE I WAS VERY ANGRY, UPSET, OR IN CONFLICT WERE:

(1) _____

(2) _____

BODY WARNING SIGNS:

IN ANGRY, UPSET, OR CONFLICT SITUATIONS *MY BODY* RESPONDS IN THESE WAYS:

(1) _____

(2) _____

(3) _____

FEELING WARNING SIGNS:

IN ANGRY, UPSET, OR CONFLICT SITUATIONS *I FEEL*:   (Use the negative feelings list)

_____

_____

_____

The Feeling That Most Often Gets Covered Up And Turned Into Anger Is:

THINKING WARNING SIGNS:

IN ANGRY, UPSET, OR CONFLICT SITUATIONS *I THINK* : (Say To Myself or Picture)

(1) _____

_____

(2) _____

_____

(3) _____

_____

(4) _____

_____

© Clyde M. Feldman and David Harvey, 1992

Clyde M. Feldman, Ph.D.

ANGER MANAGING ATTITUDE WORKSHEET

Our angry feelings signals that something's wrong and that we should take some kind of action. What kind of action we take and whether it's constructive or destructive (even violent or abusive) has a lot to do with the automatic thoughts and pictures which go through our head as we're getting **HOTTER**. If we aren't aware of these thoughts and pictures we can't change them and they become "automatic" thinking, which lead to automatic actions.

People often say "I wasn't really thinking" in angry, frustrating, and upsetting situations. When we're filled with high amounts of adrenaline and tension, our thinking can become fuzzy and seem out of our control. But our thoughts are always active even if we aren't aware of them. All angry situations are preceded by some thoughts or mental pictures we have about the situation, the other person, ourselves, and what we're going to do or say. What you say to yourself and picture will ultimately become the internal directions you give to yourself about how to feel about the situation and what to do about it.

There are four steps you can follow to become an "expert" on your own personal **HOT** thoughts and images. The more of these you can remember, the more control you'll begin to have over how you deal with any angry, frustrating, or provoking situations or arguments.

STEP 1

Try and recall any **HOT** thoughts - which may include words, beliefs, attitudes, expectations, and assumptions that went through your mind during the most recent angry situations or arguments. Also try and recall any **HOT** mental images that you remember seeing it in your mind's eye.

1. _____

_____

2. _____

_____

3. _____

_____

4. _____

_____

5. _____

_____

STEP 2

Check yourself out by answering some questions about your own automatic thoughts and pictures from above.

- **Do my HOT thoughts and pictures increase or decrease my ability to constructively solve the problem?** ☐ Increase ☐ Decrease

- **Do my HOT thoughts and pictures increase or decrease my ability to stay physically and mentally calm?** ☐ Increase ☐ Decrease

- **Do my HOT thoughts and pictures increase or decrease my ability to think clearly and stay focused on what I wanted to accomplish?** ☐ Increase ☐ Decrease

- **Do my HOT thoughts and pictures tell me to use more or less forceful techniques to deal with the situation.** ☐ More ☐ Less

- **Do my HOT thoughts and pictures make it more likely or less likely that I'll talk things out?** ☐ More ☐ Less

- **Do my HOT thoughts and pictures seem more negative and dramatic then the original situation?** ☐ Yes ☐ No

- **Was I angry, emotionally abusive, or aggressive with someone who is actually out to cause me serious harm?** ☐ Yes ☐ No

STEP 3

People can use their automatic self-talk and pictures as a signal to themselves to try out cool counter-thoughts and pictures. With practice, these counter-thought and images will lead to anger-managing attitudes and actions. Below are some examples of counter-thoughts and pictures people have developed to successfully handle angry situations and arguments by the anger-managing ATTITUDE they decided to take.

ANGRY THOUGHTS AND PICTURES	COUNTER THOUGHTS AND PICTURES
"When you interrupt me, it infuriates me!"	"I'm over-reacting again. Don't take it so personally."
"Why can't he understand!"	"How can I communicate better? I can't let my anger get in the way of talking this through."
"I want out! I want a divorce!"	"What can I do to work this out? I don't really want a divorce."
"Leave me alone!"	"I need time to think, but the way I do it only pushes him away."
"Don't lie to me!"	"I feel hurt, not angry. I can handle this if I don't start feeling like a failure."
"Why is he do doing this to me again?"	'I've heard this before…I don't have to get this upset every new time."
"She is so wrong, why can't she see it!"	"What she's saying could be true, and I need to admit that to myself."
"Lay off, damn it!"	"I need to calm down and take time to think. I need to try to understand how he's feeling."
"I can see myself putting my hands on her shoulders and holding her down."	"I can see a picture of how I'd want this argument to turn out instead. I see myself being able to walk away."
"She's cold to me and makes me feel rejected all the time!"	"Quit adding fuel to the fire. I need to really understand why she's acting so cold."
"He does this to me to mess with my mind!"	"I know that's not true. He just doesn't know to deal with me at these times."
"She deserves to be hit!"	"Nobody deserves to be hit. I don't have to solve this right now, there's tine to talk."

Imagine yourself substituting a cool thought or mental image that would be a powerful reminder of how to help stay in control and manage the situation the way you would like to. Try and come up with one counter-statement or picture for each **HOT** thought or picture one you wrote down in STEP 1 that is powerful enough to counteract it.

1. _____

2. _____

3. _____

4. _____

5. _____

STEP 4

Go back to STEP 2 and see if you would answer the same questions differently for each of these new counter thoughts and pictures.

© Clyde M. Feldman, 1994

THE ADVANTAGES VERSUS THE DISADVANTAGES OF ANGER AND FIGHTING

Many times we don't realize that getting angry and getting into fights and arguments can have both ADVANTAGES and DISADVANTAGES. It's usually easiest to think of the negative consequences and negative costs associated with being angry and fighting. For example, the loss of trust and closeness, broken objects, etc. But getting angry and fighting may actually have HIDDEN advantages and payoffs that we may not be very aware of. For example, for some people the payoffs have included getting even, blowing off steam, hoping it will finally get the other person to change some behavior, being "right", having power or control over the other person, punishing the other person, defending your self-image, and making-up.

First, it's important to IDENTIFY what the personal disadvantages and advantages are for you in getting angry and fighting. Then, you can see how the disadvantages and advantages STACK UP against each other.

DISADVANTAGES OF ANGER AND FIGHTING

LIST THE DISADVANTAGES, NEGATIVE CONSEQUENCES, PUNISHERS, NEGATIVE COSTS, DISSATISFACTIONS, AND LOSSES ASSOCIATED WITH BEING ANGRY AND FIGHTING.

1. _____
2. _____
3. _____
4. _____
5. _____
6. _____

ADVANTAGES OF ANGER AND FIGHTING

LIST THE ADVANTAGES, POSITIVE CONSEQUENCES, PAYOFFS, SATISFACTIONS, REWARDS, REINFORCERS, AND BENEFITS ASSOCIATED WITH BEING ANGRY AND FIGHTING.

1. _____
2. _____
3. _____
4. _____
5. _____
6. _____

© Clyde M. Feldman, 1994

SIX TYPES OF HOT THOUGHTS THAT ESCALATE ANGER AND UPSET

1. **LABELING** Categorizing someone in a totally negative manner. Rather than recognizing that the person you're angry at is a complex mixture of both positive and negative qualities, we reduce them to a single most negative label. For example, instead of thinking "They made a mistake", you think: "That jerk", "Shit-head", "Idiot, "She's just a whore", "He's a loser", "She's a total bitch".

2. **MIND-READING** Jumping to conclusions - by assuming that you know what the other person was thinking and why they acted the way they did without any real evidence and without really checking it out with them. We usually decide that the person's behavior was on purpose, their intention was negative, and they were out to cause us harm. For example: "She did it on purpose", "She knows I can't stand that", "She's doing it to get back at me", "He's probably cheating on me, that's why he's acting so nice", "This is her little way of making me admit I was wrong."

3. **FORTUNE-TELLING** Jumping to conclusions - by assuming that you know what will happen in the future and how things will turn out because of what's happened before or because you believe nothing can ever change. We usually predict only negative things will happen. For example: "She'll never change", "He's always been like this and he always will", "There's no use in trying".

4. **BLACK & WHITE THINKING** Looking at situations and people in black-and-white categories... no middle-ground grey area. Mentally, we use words like "all" or "nothing", "never" or "always", "success" or "failure". For example: "She never appreciates anything I ever do", She always rejects me", All men are alike, they only care about themselves", "She's always late", "I'm a failure".

5. **MAGNIFYING** Blowing things way out of proportion and over-exaggerating their importance, seriousness, or consequences. Usually we do this because we are taking things too personally. Rather than being mildly annoyed over something, we convince ourselves that it is terrible, awful, horrible. Then we often decide to do something dramatic about it. For example: "I can't stand this any longer", "If he puts me down one more time, I'll lock him out of the house", "I have to shut her up anyway I can".

6. **DEMANDING** Turning our wants into "Shoulds" and "Musts" and "Have Tos". This leads to a sense of injustice and self-righteous anger, and finally to a desire for vengeance. It's not just a preference, it's a law or rule. For example: "She shouldn't act that way", "He has to go tonight", "They should do it this way".

Modified and expanded from David Burns, 1980

PREPARING FOR AND HANDLING ANGRY SITUATIONS

PREPARING EARLY BEFORE THINGS GET HEATED UP

What exactly do I have to do to handle this the way I want to?
Just think rationally. My negative thoughts aren't very rational.
I can work out a plan to handle this without losing it.
I get better with practice.
I'm going to get through this ok.
If I start getting upset, I'll remind myself what I need to do.
This is going to upset me, but I can deal with it.
Don't take this so seriously and so personally.
This could be a nasty situation, but I have to believe in myself.
There won't be any need to get verbally or physically aggressive.
Remember how I want to think about this tomorrow.
I need to know when to leave and take a time-out.

HANDLING THE ACTUAL SITUATION WITHOUT GETTING PROVOKED

Stay calm and breath. I don't need to lose control here.
I'm controlling my anger for myself, not just for the other person.
I've been in this kind a situation a 100 times before, so why do I let it get to me?
I've got to quit adding fuel to the fire.
They aren't at their best and neither am I.
As long as I keep my cool, I'll stay in control.
Just roll with the punches, don't get all bent out of shape.
I can leave like I planned.
Remember what I want to get out of this.
I don't need to prove anything.
There's no point in getting mad.
I don't have to solve this right now. There's time to handle it later.
Don't make more out of this than I have to.
I'm over-reacting again. Don't take everything so personally.
I need to talk it out, not fight it out.
What can I do to work this out?
I need time to think and calm down.

I'm not going to let them get to me.
I've got to be responsible for my buttons getting pushed, not them.
Stop assuming the worst and jumping to conclusions.
It's really a shame that they have to act like this.
For someone to act that way, they really have to be unhappy.
If I start to get mad, I'll just be banging my own head against the wall.
There's no need to take it so personally and start feeling bad about myself.
If I blow up, I could lose things and people that are important to me.
I can't let what they say get to me. It doesn't really matter.
I can't change them with anger.
I'm on top of this situation and in control of myself.
I need to relax and slow things down.
Getting this upset won't help anything.
It's just not worth it to get this angry.
I'll end up looking like the one with the problem.
I have a right to be upset, but I have to keep the lid on.
It's time to take a time-out, disengage, and back off.
I need to stay cool and rational.
My anger should remind me of what I want to do instead.
I'm not going to get pushed around, but I'm not going haywire either.
I have to try to reason things out.
I need to stay respectful even if they aren't.
I have to stay away from a Win-Lose, Right-Wrong attitude.
It's not me against them. It's not some battle to the "death".
They'd probably like to see me lose it, but I'm going to disappoint them.
I can't expect people to act the way I want them to.
Take it easy... Slow down... think about what you're doing.
Forget about the aggravation... Thinking about it only makes me more upset.
I can't solve this right now. I need to take a break and calm down.
Try to shake it off.
I need to practice doing the opposite, even though it doesn't feel like me.
Take a deep breath.
Don't take it so personally.
Don't let my pride get in the way.

GIVING MYSELF SOME CREDIT

I handled that better than I would have before.
That went better than I thought.
It could have been a lot worse.
I actually got through that without losing it.
I've been getting upset for a long time, when it isn't really necessary.
I can be proud of this instead of feeling bad about myself.
I can tell that I'm getting some trust back.
I can see that other people are noticing a difference in me.

© Clyde M. Feldman, 2005

EIGHT CHARACTERISTICS OF ABUSIVE HOMES

1. **DENIAL:** Keep secrets from other members. Minimize or deny what recently happened or the seriousness of it. Make excuses for the negative things. If you say something or confront the situation, you're not believed, listened to, or are punished.

2. **INCONSISTENCY / UNPREDICTABILITY:** Routines or rituals are inconsistent. Rules were unclear or kept sometimes, broken other times. Can't rely on people in charge to do what, or be where, they said they would. Parents' emotional reactions are differed on different days and/or with different kids.

3. **LACK OF EMPATHY:** Parents are insensitive, not comforting nor understanding, disapproving, or ridicule how you feel. Parents have unrealistic expectations of you and when they weren't met, responded either in B&W terms or with anger/aggression or with withdraw.

4. **LACK OF CLEAR BOUNDARIES:** (a) *Physical*: not respecting your privacy, personal possessions or your body; (b) *Psychological*: making you do things that you didn't want to, teasing, belittling, sexual innuendos, etc.

5. **ROLE REVERSAL:** Parents don't show leadership, or set limits, or act appropriately in charge. Kids may have to take over/take on parent- tasks. Kids may have to take care of parents logistically or emotionally.

6. **CLOSED SYSTEM:** Few ties to community activities, social network, no friends over. What goes on in the house is private. You or parents don't want others to see what goes on in house.

7. **MIXED MESSAGES:** Real message is confusing because words, nonverbals, and actions don't match (e.g., I hit you because I love you. They say they're proud of you, but act angry at you; Tell you to go help your dad, then is jealous that you did).

8. **AGGRESSIVE CONFLICT OR CONFLICT AVOIDANCE:** Intense fights, explosive anger, or disagreements and upset are kept bottled up and suppressed (e.g., dirty looks, negative silences, issues fester).

Summary based upon Steven Farmer, 1996

EIGHT IMPACTS OF CHILDHOOD ABUSE ON THE PERSON AS AN ADULT

1. **LACK OF TRUST:** Are highly cautious of people and assume that they will reject you, hurt you, get angry and not understand and not listen to what you think and feel. So you: (1) see people in black-and-white terms as either "can or can't be trusted", (2) don't disclose what you truly think or feel, (3) wait a long time before someone is "safe", (4) are always on the lookout for violations of trust, and (5) assume a negative event means more than it does.

2. **AVOIDING FEELINGS:** Deny, repress, minimize, cover-up normal feelings and reactions, both negative (angry, sad) and positive (joy), especially intense feelings. Feelings sometimes get expressed in either indirect ways (passive-aggressive, complaining) or in an intense release that involves acting them out (blow-up, fall apart, "drama").

3. **LOW SELF-ESTEEM:** Form conclusions about yourself that you're stupid, clumsy, bad, ugly, worthless, unlovable, you'll never be. .no one will ever. .and *act as* if these are true. In relationships, you may find someone who fulfills the belief you're not ok. In work, you may be competitive/driven -or- the opposite and fear/avoid success.

4. **SENSE OF HELPLESSNESS / DEPRESSION:** May maintain a passive, helpless, powerless, victimized stance to life and that you have little or no control/influence over things/people. May develop chronic feelings of depression along with unexpressed rage.

5. **DIFFICULTIES WITH RELATIONSHIPS:** (1) overly distant and independent, (2) overly clingy, dependent, intense, (3) tests others constantly, (4) pick abusive partners, [create your own rejection]

6. **ALCOHOL/DRUG PROBLEMS:** Increased risk to ease emotional pain and discomfort in various intimate or social situations.

7. **EATING-RELATED PROBLEMS:** Increased risk related to dislike of self, body image, attempts to control their world.

8. **ANXIETY PROBLEMS:** Increased risk of PTSD (i.e., anxiety, disassociation, get triggered in similar situations, flashbacks). Also have other anxieties.

Summary based upon Steven Farmer, 1996

SECTION 4:

DEPRESSION TOOLS

Clyde M. Feldman, Ph.D.

DEPRESSION INVENTORY

NAME: _____   DATE: _____

This questionnaire consists of 21 groups of statements. Please read each group of statements carefully, and then pick out the one statement in each group that best describes the way you have been feeling during the past two weeks, including today. Circle the number beside the statement you have picked. If several statements in the group seem to apply equally well, circle the highest number for that group. Be sure that you do not choose more than one statement for any group. including item 16 (changes in sleeping pattern) or item 18 (changes in appetite).

1. **SADNESS**
    - 0   I do not feel sad.
    - 1   I feel sad much of the time.
    - 2   I am sad all the time.
    - 3   I am so sad or unhappy that I can't stand it.

2. **PESSIMISM**
    - 0   I am not discouraged about my future.
    - 1   I feel more discouraged about my future than I used to be.
    - 2   I do not expect things to work out for me.
    - 3   I feel my future is hopeless and will only get worse.

3. **PAST FAILURE**
    - 0   I do not feel like a failure.
    - 1   I have failed more than I should have.
    - 2   As I look back, I see a lot of failures.
    - 3   I feel I am a total failure as a person.

4. **LOSS OF PLEASURE**
    - 0   I get as much pleasure as I ever did from the things I enjoy.
    - 1   I don't enjoy things as much as I used to.
    - 2   I get very little pleasure from the things I used to enjoy.
    - 3   I can't get any pleasure from the things I used to enjoy.

5. **GUILTY FEELINGS**
   - 0   I don't feel particularly guilty.
   - 1   I feel guilty over many things I have done or should have done.
   - 2   I feel quite guilty most of the time.
   - 3   I feel guilty all of the time.

6. **PUNISHMENT FEELINGS**
   - 0   I don't feel I am being punished.
   - 1   I feel I may be punished.
   - 2   I expect to be punished.
   - 3   I feel I am being punished.

7. **SELF-DISLIKE**
   - 0   I feel the same about myself as ever.
   - 1   I have lost confidence in myself.
   - 2   I am disappointed in myself.
   - 3   I dislike myself.

8. **SELF-CRITICALNESS**
   - 0   I don't criticize or blame myself more than usual.
   - 1   I am more critical of myself than I used to be.
   - 2   I criticize myself for all of my faults.
   - 3   I blame myself for everything bad that happens.

9. **SUICIDAL THOUGHTS OR WISHES**
   - 0   I don't have any thoughts of killing myself.
   - 1   I have thoughts of killing myself, but I would not carry them out.
   - 2   I would like to kill myself.
   - 3   I would kill myself if I had the chance.

10. **CRYING**
    - 0   I don't cry anymore than I used to.
    - 1   I cry more than I used to.
    - 2   I cry over every little thing.
    - 3   I feel like crying, but I can't.

11. **AGITATION**
    - 0   I am no more restless or wound up than usual.
    - 1   I feel more restless or wound up than usual.
    - 2   I am so restless or agitated that it's hard to stay still.
    - 3   I am so restless or agitated that I have to keep moving or doing something.

12. **LOSS OF INTEREST**
    0   I have not lost interest in other people or activities.
    1   I am less interested in other people or things than before.
    2   I have lost most of my interest in other people or things.
    3   It's hard to get interested in anything.

13. **INDECISIVENESS**
    0   I make decisions about as well as ever.
    1   I find it more difficult to make decisions than usual.
    2   I have much greater difficulty in making decision than I used to.
    3   I have trouble making any decisions.

14. **WORTHLESSNESS**
    0   I do not feel I am worthless.
    1   I don't consider myself as worthwhile and useful as I used to.
    2   I feel more worthless as compared to other people.
    3   I feel utterly worthless.

15. **LOSS OF ENERGY**
    0   I have as much energy as ever.
    1   I have less energy than I used to have.
    2   I don't have enough energy to do very much.
    3   I don't have enough energy to do anything.

16. **CHANGES IN SLEEPING PATTERN**
    0   I have not experienced any change in my sleeping pattern.
    1   I sleep somewhat more than usual OR I sleep somewhat less than usual.
    2   I sleep a lot more than usual OR I sleep a lot less than usual.
    3   I sleep most of the day OR I wake up 1-2 hours early and can't get back to sleep.

17. **IRRITABILITY**
    0   I am no more irritable than usual.
    1   I am more irritable than usual.
    2   I am much more irritable than usual.
    3   I am irritable all the time.

18. **CHANGES IN APPETITE**
    0   I have not experienced any change in my appetite.
    1   My appetite is somewhat less than usual OR somewhat greater than usual.
    2   My appetite is much less than before OR much greater than usual.
    3   I have no appetite at all OR I crave food all the time.

19. **CONCENTRATION DIFFICULTY**
    - 0   I can concentrate as well as ever.
    - 1   I can't concentrate as well as usual.
    - 2   It's hard to keep my mind on anything for very long.
    - 3   I find I can't concentrate on anything.

20. **TIREDNESS OR FATIGUE**
    - 0   I am no more tired or fatigued than usual.
    - 1   I get more tired or fatigued more easily than usual.
    - 2   I am too tired or fatigued to do a lot of the things that I used to do.
    - 3   I am too tired or fatigued to do most of the things I used to do.

21. **LOSS OF INTEREST IN SEX**
    - 0   I have not noticed any recent change in my interest in sex.
    - 1   I am less interested in sex than I used to be.
    - 2   I am much less interested in sex now.
    - 3   I have lost interest in sex completely.

SCORING

ADD UP THE SCORES FOR ALL 21 ITEMS _____ .

- **0-13 =**   MOST LIKELY NOT CLINICALLY DEPRESSED
- **14-19 =** MOST LIKELY MILDLY DEPRESSED
- **20-28 =** MOST LIKELY MODERATELY DEPRESSED
- **29-63 =** MOST LIKELY SEVERELY DEPRESSED

© Aaron T. Beck, Robert A. Steer, Gregory K. Brown, 1996

Clyde M. Feldman, Ph.D.

BIPOLAR QUESTIONNAIRE

HAS THERE EVER BEEN A PERIOD OF TIME WHEN YOU WERE
<u>NOT YOUR USUAL SELF</u> AND .....

	Yes	No
1. You felt so good, enthusiastic, optimistic, or euphoric that people that know you thought it wasn't normal or was extreme or excessive?	☐	☐
2. You were so irritable that you made complaints, hostile comments, angry rants, or started fights/arguments, especially when others didn't agree, or understand, or go along with what you wanted?	☐	☐
3. You felt so self-confident that you thought about and/or did things that you might not realistically have enough experience or skill at, like giving specific advice, starting a company, writing a novel, or inventing something?	☐	☐
4. You needed much less sleep than usual and when you got much less sleep you found you weren't tired or didn't miss it?	☐	☐
5. You talked much more, or spoke much faster or louder than usual?	☐	☐
6. Your thoughts were racing through your head, maybe even faster than you could put into words, or you couldn't slow your mind down?	☐	☐
7. You were easily distracted by things around you, so you had trouble concentrating or staying on track?	☐	☐
8. You had much more energy than usual?	☐	☐
9. You were involved in planning and/or doing many more activities or projects than usual, particularly all going on at the same time?	☐	☐
10. You were much more social than usual, like contacting friends, people you haven't talked to, or even public figures or the media?	☐	☐
11. Your sexual drive, sexual fantasies, and/or sexual activities were much more frequent or stronger than usual?	☐	☐

12. You did things that other people thought were unusual for you and may have thought were excessive, risky, or foolish? ☐ ☐

13. You engaged in things that seemed fine or pleasurable at the time but were probably excessive, risky, or foolish in terms of spending money, driving, business, socializing, or engaging in sexual activities, etc.? ☐ ☐

14. If you checked YES to two or more of the above, has more than one of these happened during the same period of time? ☐ ☐

15. How much of a problem did any of these cause you - like being unable to work, having family, money, or legal troubles, or getting into arguments or fights?

    No problem ☐   Minor Problem ☐   Moderate problem ☐   Serious Problem ☐

Yes   No

16. Have any of your blood relatives had manic-depression or bipolar disorder (children, siblings, parents, grandparents, aunts, uncles)? ☐ ☐

17. Has a healthcare professional ever told you that you have manic-depression or bipolar disorder? ☐ ☐

SCORING:

YOU HAVE A HIGH PROBABILITY OF HAVING A BI-POLAR PROBLEM IF:

YOU CHECKED YES ON 7 OR MORE ITEMS FROM 1-13 AND...

YOU CHECKED YES ON ITEM 14 AND...

YOU CHECKED "MODERATE" OR "SERIOUS" ON ITEM 15.

DEPRESSED THINKING IS DEPRESSING

Depression brings with it an overly negative view and interpretation of yourself, of the world, and of the future. This thinking traps you and ends up creating feelings of sadness, discouragement, helplessness, hopelessness, worthlessness, and guilt.

- **A Negative View of Yourself**: You begin to think about yourself as inadequate, defective, undesirable, worthless, incompetent, inept, fatally flawed, or deficient in the attributes you value most (likability, intelligence, etc.). You begin to be very self-critical and underestimate your own ability to have a positive impact on situations. People that are depressed have had thoughts about themselves like:

  - It's my fault when things go wrong or when other people around me start to have problems.
  - There's not one thing about me that's really special or unique.
  - I'm not living up to my potential.
  - I have to be successful in whatever I undertake.
  - I make a mess of every job.
  - If I make a mistake, it means I'm inept or a failure.
  - I should be making more money every year to be successful.
  - I'm different than other people because I'm fatally flawed.
  - Why am I so weak?
  - Why do I keep pushing men/women away when I know better?
  - I'm worse than my mother... I'm not fit to be a parent.
  - I've never been good at anything.
  - Bad things matter much more than good things.
  - I'm a reject.
  - I ruined my kids life because I divorced.
  - I don't really have anything to offer.
  - If I feel stupid this often, I must be stupid.
  - I shouldn't feel jealous, sad, guilty, etc....what's wrong with me?

- **A Negative View of Others/the World**: You begin to think about others and the world as making extreme demands on you and placing insurmountable obstacles in your way. You begin to see the world and others as depriving you of what other people seem to get, rejecting you, or socially isolating you. People that are depressed have had thoughts about the world and other people like:

   - People should never dislike me, disagree with me, or disapprove of me because that means that they hate me and reject me.
   - I can't live without (some person) or I'll just fall apart or die.
   - I have to be nice, give up things, pretend to make things go well.
   - I'm so lonely but no one would want to be with me the way I am.
   - They're deeply disappointed in me but would never tell me.
   - They don't really love me, they're just pretending to not hurt my feelings.
   - Everybody finds friends but me.
   - I have to pretend to be ok If I'm going to keep my friends.
   - They'd be better off if I was dead.
   - I'm not part of anything... I have no sense of family.
   - They're just giving me an interview because they know my father.
   - They think I'm a basket case.
   - If they don't want me, who else would.
   - I know by the way they looked at their watch, that they thought I was totally boring.
   - If I'd done a better job as a father, my son wouldn't be married to a witch now.
   - Good jobs come to people who are really competent, you don't have to go looking for them like I do.
   - My husband/wife doesn't really care about me or they would want to help me more.
   - Things should turn out the way I want to turn out.

- **A Negative View of the Future**: You begin to see the future as being forever difficult and painful - indefinitely. Any attempts at trying to change that are hopeless because you will fail. You start to think that everything is going to be so hard and overwhelming and turn out so badly that there's no point in even trying. People that are depressed have had thoughts about the future like:

    - You have to focus on the worst case scenario, because that's the one that's likely to happen.
    - What if's...What if it turns out to be hard/bad, which it no doubt will.
    - If it's been true in the past, it's always going to be true.
    - I'll be alone forever.
    - I'll never find a good job.
    - I'll always be depressed.
    - I'll never get over ____.
    - I'll always be this way.
    - The next time is going to turn out badly just like the last time.

© Clyde M. Feldman, 2000

16 WAYS TO RE-EVALUATE WHAT YOU SAY TO YOURSELF

1. What's the hard evidence for this being true? Have you really tested it out fully or did you just decide to <u>accept</u> it as true?

2. Does this hold true 100% of the time and in 100% of situations?

3. Do others agree with what you say to yourself and think it's healthy?

4. Has this always been true? Have you ever done anything in your life that was an exception to this or that contradicted this?

5. Is what you say to yourself flexible, does it have exceptions, and does it have grey areas or is it totally black and white, rigid, with no exceptions?

6. Who says? Compared to what? Compared to who? Based on what standard? Who decided that standard?

7. Is believing this good for you? Does it make you feel <u>better</u> about yourself, more in <u>control</u> of your life, better able to <u>cope</u> -or- does it make you feel worse, less in control, and less able to cope?

8. Does this keep you focused on the big picture, or does it keep you focused on one narrow aspect of things... like tunnel vision?

9. Do this make you <u>over</u>-emphasize and exaggerate the negative things and make you <u>under</u>-emphasize and minimize the positive things?

10. Is your rational, logical, and objective side telling you this -or- is it all based on intense feelings and emotions?

11. Is this something you <u>decided</u> to think and believe on your own, or did you get it from the past or from people like parents, etc.?

12. If you had a best friend in your situation, would you take the same attitude about <u>them</u> and <u>their situation</u> that you do about <u>yours</u>?

13. Image someone who's more like the way you wish you could be? Would they be saying the same things to themself as you do?

14. If you could magically get rid of this or take it less personally and less seriously, what would you be able to do, to feel, to believe, and to handle that you can't now?

15. What's the worst that could actually happen and how likely is that?

16. What would happen if you could stop saying this to yourself? Who's stopping you?

Modified and expanded from Robert Leahy & Stephen Holland, 2000

NEGATIVE REACTION WORKSHEET FOR DEPRESSION

SITUATION: Describe the situation. It may be one where you were by yourself or with others.

_____

_____

NEGATIVE FEELINGS: List as many as you had in the situation (sad, hopeless, rejected, hurt, worthless) and also rate the intensity from 1 (low) to 10 (high)

_____

_____

_____

AUTOMATIC THOUGHTS: Write down the negative thoughts, beliefs, assumptions, expectations, and mental pictures that were going through your mind about yourself, other people, the situation, the future, etc. Also rate your belief in each of these from 1% (not really) to 100% (completely)

_____

_____

_____

_____

OUTCOME: How did your automatic thoughts end up making you feel worse about yourself, other people, or the future.

_____

_____

FOUR WAYS TO HELP CREATE POSITIVE SELF-TALK AND POSITIVE MENTAL PICTURES

YOUR POSITIVE PAST EXPERIENCE

Remember, think of, or find a time in the past, in a similar kind of situation, when you were able to handle things more like you want to now. Remember that now and put yourself back into that situation. What were you able to say to yourself, believe, remind yourself, picture to yourself, feel emotionally, and do back then that would help you in the current situation?

FUTURE PROJECTION

Imagine that you could project yourself into the future (__ months / years from now), at a point in time when you have already figured out how to handle this kind of situation. What are you able to say to yourself, believe, remind yourself, picture to yourself, feel emotionally, and do in the future that would help you in the present?

A COACH OR MODEL

Think about someone - real or fictional, public or you know personally, living or passed away - who knows how to handle this kind of situation the way you wish you could. What would they coach you to say to yourself, believe, remind yourself, picture to yourself, feel emotionally, and do in the current situation? What would they be able to do say to themselves, picture, or do that you could try out for yourself?

A MAGIC WAND

Imagine you had a magic wand and you could use it on yourself to handle this kind of situation they way you wish you could. What would it give you the ability to say to yourself, believe, remind yourself, picture to yourself, feel emotionally, and do in this situation?

© Adapted from NLP and Solution-focused models by Clyde M. Feldman, 2010

POSITIVE COUNTER-STATEMENTS AND PICTURES WORKSHEET FOR REDUCING DEPRESSION

WRITE DOWN YOUR NEGATIVE THOUGHTS, BELIEFS, ASSUMPTIONS, EXPECTATIONS, AND MENTAL PICTURES WHEN DEPRESSED:

1a. _____

2a. _____

3a. _____

4a. _____

CREATE A POSITIVE COUNTER-STATEMENT, POSITIVE COPING STATEMENT, OR POSITIVE MENTAL PICTURE FOR EACH OF THE ABOVE:

1b. _____

2b. _____

3b. _____

4b. _____

QUESTIONS TO IDENTIFY POSITIVES AND STRENGTHS

What do you think are some of your best qualities?

What do you like best about yourself?

What do other people like about you?

What are some things you're proud of?

What's one of the tougher things you've pulled off well?

What's one of the best things you've ever done for yourself or for somebody else?

When you're at your very best, what are your special talents, skills or abilities?

Describe one or two important things you've ever learned in your life.

What are you better at now than you used to be?

How do you make yourself feel happy or content or peaceful?

What's the best advice you've given someone?

What positive things would you want a stranger to know about you?

What's your favorite compliment that you've ever received?

Describe the best thing(s) about your family, your job, and your friends.

In this situation, what are you doing that's helping, or at least keeping it from getting worse?

In this situation, what are you doing better now than you used to do?

© Clyde M. Feldman, 2004

IDENTIFICATION AND RANKING OF PLEASURABLE ACTIVITIES

ACTIVITY OR EVENT (done alone or with others)	AMOUNT OF PLEASURE (from 1 to 100)	HOW OFTEN/WK DO YOU DO IT?

© Clyde M. Feldman, 2004

POSSIBLE ACTIVITIES TO IMPROVE DEPRESSION

Activities	Have tried successfully	Should use more often	Would like to try
Exercise			
Sports (such as basketball, soccer, volleyball)			
Long walks			
Yoga			
Dancing			
Reading			
Listening to music			
Long, hot baths			
Making love			
Gardening			
Long drives			
Needlework			
Working with wood			
Working with clay, pottery			
Drawing, painting			
Journal writing			
Writing poetry			
Writing letters			
Canoeing			
Horseback riding			
Shopping			
Relaxing in a meditative natural setting			
Day trips			
Playing a musical instrument			

Spending time with young children			
Cleaning			
Watching a funny movie			
Watching TV			
Watching a movie, or going to a concert or play			
Buying something I've been wanting			
Helping others			

Support	Have tried successfully	Should use more often	Would like to try
Talking it out with an understanding person			
Getting emotional support from a person I trust			
Talking to a therapist or counselor			
Peer counseling			
Talking to people who validate my feelings			
Spending time with good friends			
Talking to staff at a crisis clinic or hotline			
Arranging not to be alone			.
Reaching out to someone			
Being held by someone I love			
Going to a support group			
Spending time with and taking responsibility for a pet			

Attitude	Have tried successfully	Should use more often	Would like to try
Changing negative thought patterns to positive ones			
Waiting it out			
Staying active			
Remembering that depression ends			

Recalling good times			
Being good to myself			
Diverting my attention			
Being gentle with myself			
Refusing to feel guilty			
Focusing on living one day at a time			
Endorsing and affirming my efforts			
Laughter			

Management	Have tried successfully	Should use more often	Would like to try
Medication			
Full-spectrum light			
Spending time outside			
Keeping busy			
Eating a diet high in complex carbohydrates			
Eliminating foods that worsen my depression			
Resting			
Forcing myself to get up in the morning			
Forcing myself to go to work			
Doing whatever I need to do to meet my needs			
Maintaining a balance of rest and good times			

Spirituality	Have tried successfully	Should use more often	Would like to try
Praying			
Getting in touch with my spirituality			
Meditating			
Keeping up with a 12-step program			

ACTIVITY SCHEDULE FOR THIS WEEK

Rate Your Sense of Accomplishment (A) and Your Sense of Pleasure (P) from 1 to 5

1 =NONE   2 =A LITTLE   3 =A MODERATE AMOUNT   4 =A GOOD DEAL   5=A LOT

TIME	M	T	W	TH	F	SAT	SUN
7-8 am							
8-9 am							
9-10 am							
10-11am							
11-12 pm							
12-1 pm							
1-2 pm							
2-3 pm							

3-4 pm							
4-5 pm							
5-6 pm							
6-7 pm							
7-8 pm							
8-9 pm							
9-12 pm							

SECTION 5:

ANXIETY TOOLS

A MODEL OF THE FACTORS WHICH LEAD TO AND MAINTAIN ANXIETY PROBLEMS

BIOLOGICAL VULNERABILITY

- TENDENCY TO BE MORE EMOTIONALLY REACTIVE
- BIOCHEMICAL IMBALANCES OR DEFICITS

↓

EMOTIONAL INSECURITIES

- CAUTIOUS, DANGEROUS WORLD VIEW
- FEELING REJECTED, NEGLECTED
- POOR SOCIAL SKILLS

↓

FALSE ALARM

ANXIOUS OVER-REACTION TO EVENTS AND SITUATIONS WHICH ARE NOT TRULY DANGEROUS

↓

LEARNED RESPONSES THAT MAINTAIN OR INCREASE THE FALSE ALARM

- ANXIOUS SELF-TALK, MENTAL PICTURES, AND BELIEFS
- AVOIDANCE OF THE FEARED SITUATIONS OR OBJECTS
- COMPULSIVE BEHAVIORS
- PARTNER IS <u>NON</u>-SUPPORTIVE OR <u>OVERLY</u>-SUPPORTIVE

DESCRIPTION OF THE MODEL FOR ANXIETY PROBLEMS

Although each person's anxiety problem has a different origin, there is a general model about how and why anxiety problems start and what tends to maintain or even increase them. The model on the previous page is based on extensive research by David Barlow and his colleagues. The model of how anxiety works is explained below.

BIOLOGICAL VULNERABILITY

- TENDENCY TO BE MORE EMOTIONALLY REACTIVE

Some evidence of inherited vulnerability, tendency, or predisposition towards: (1) "nervousness", (2) a more "excitable" autonomic nervous system, (3) a stronger attention to "threat", and (4) a tendency to withdraw from unfamiliar situations. That "tendency" appears to be activated under stressful situations. A person is four times more likely to have an anxiety problem if a first-degree relative has it. This is most true for OCD, panic, and specific phobias. It is less true for generalized anxiety disorder and PTSD.

- BIOCHEMICAL IMBALANCES OR DEFICITS

Possible imbalances or deficits in neurotransmitter levels and/or hormone levels. Also a central nervous system monitor that is oversensitive to "suffocation" via elevated levels of carbon dioxide (can make people have an attack with increased levels of carbon dioxide).

↓

EMOTIONAL INSECURITIES

- CAUTIOUS, DANGEROUS WORLD VIEW

An overly cautious view of the world communicated to a child by parents/family who may be more fearful and anxious than average themselves. "Don't go out in rain, you'll catch cold", "Don't play in dirt, you'll get germs"... *Be very careful* messages which encourage a view of world as a dangerous place and restricting one's exploration and risk-taking.

- **FEELING REJECTED, NEGLECTED**

Issues of childhood neglect, rejection, abandonment, abuse, shame, and guilt. May have experienced overtly negative interactions via divorce, deaths, or illness. Created feeling of emotional dependency in response to insecurity.

- **POOR SOCIAL SKILLS**

Poorer communication (i.e., talks less, poor or weird eye contact, self-discloses less, expresses opinions less, seems less enthusiastic and less genuine) poorer assertiveness skills, and less able to read others and their emotions.

↓

FALSE ALARM

ANXIOUS OVER-REACTION TO EVENTS AND SITUATIONS WHICH ARE NOT TRULY DANGEROUS

↓

LEARNED RESPONSES THAT MAINTAIN OR INCREASE THE FALSE ALARM

- **ANXIOUS SELF-TALK, BELIEFS, AND MENTAL PICTURES**

Individuals create a wide range of anxious self-talk, anxious mental images, and anxious beliefs which make assumptions, presumptions, expectations, and anticipations about how likely the next occurrence will be, how catastrophic the outcome will be, and how unable they will be to cope with and manage the situation, event, or object.

• AVOIDANCE OF THE FEARED SITUATIONS OR OBJECTS

Avoidance tends to get increasingly reinforced and strengthened because it reduces anxiety, at least initially. Avoidance also serves to keep the person from realizing that their reaction is a "False Alarm" rather than being valid and necessary ("True Alarm").

(PATTERNS OF SELF-TALK AND AVOIDANCE)

The common ways in which self-talk/pictures/beliefs and avoidance operate with anxiety problems are described below.

PANIC: Self-talk validates the belief that the physical sensations are dangerous or life threatening thereby getting the person more and more panicky (hyperventilate, etc.). The person anticipates future attacks and the fear of having another attack becomes their biggest fear. Avoidance of situations where a person can't get help easily or would feel humiliated can ultimately limit their ability to function normally and may lead to Agoraphobic behavior.

GENERALIZED ANXIETY DISORDER: Worry increases stress which decreases the person's ability to cope with stressors. It may also lower their positive sense of self which only aggravates the more core and global fears underlying GAD such as fear of failure, rejection, not being in control, or not being good enough or perfect. Avoidance is often related to worrying in such a way as to distract oneself or "worry shift" before one can fully evaluate the realistic outcome or their realistic ability to cope with the outcome.

SOCIAL ANXIETY: Self-talk leads to increased levels of anxiety which then leads to doing or saying things that ultimately are embarrassing or socially awkward (e.g., forget during public speaking). Avoidance (e.g., parties, dating) never gives the person a chance to develop and practice needed social skills and to gain confidence.

SPECIFIC PHOBIA: Self-talk validates the belief that feared situations are too dangerous to manage and that the person doesn't have the ability to cope or handle such intense stimuli. Avoidance makes it unlikely that the person will ever: (1) confront the situation in order to know it is not inherently dangerous, and (2) develop the skills and coping abilities to handle feared situations.

PTSD: Self-talk increases the likelihood that the person will re-traumatize themselves by re-experiencing all the original symptoms in response to more and more generalized triggers. Avoiding aspects of situations that remind the person of the trauma can contribute to the triggers never becoming neutralized and contributing to a belief that "I'll never get over this".

OCD: Self-talk validates that the obsessions will come true if the person doesn't do something to stop them AND validates that the obsessions cannot be gotten rid of or reduced by ordinary means but rather require compulsions to neutralize them. Also, that the person is not able to control their own thoughts and images. Avoidance in OCD is replaced with compulsive behavior. As with avoidance, enacting the compulsion makes it unlikely that the person will ever experience that the obsessions are NOT valid and will NOT come true.

- COMPULSIVE BEHAVIORS (SEE OCD)

- RELATIONSHIP RESPONSES

NON-SUPPORTIVE: Partner doesn't take the problem seriously or becomes irate, resentful, critical, or intolerant of the problem. (Examples: Fear of flying partner becomes irate and resentful that plans must be changed or cancelled; Panic partner sees that treatment for panic makes little difference and becomes fed-up, overtly critical, and intolerant which leaves person feeling more fearful, alone, and depressed; OCD partner is tired of the person's constant need for reassurance about contamination until partner stops caring; OCD partner has to wait an extra hour for person to re-check or re-wash; OCD family can't have certain foods cause person refuses to buy or cook them; GAD partner begins to stop caring and withdraws which leaves person feeling more insecure and worried).

OVERLY-SUPPORTIVE: Partner allows the problem person to become too dependent on them or enables them. (Examples: Panic partner becomes over-involved and indulges problem partner about wanting to eat more at home, not go out to movies, etc., which reinforces the agoraphobia and indirectly encourages person to give up more responsibilities; Social anxiety partner takes over by doing all the talking at parties, making excuses for him not giving the presentation, not having to eat in public restaurants which reinforces doing less and less socially; PTSD partner is very understanding about the residual affects of a sexual assault and will not pressure or push her to be sexual or close or express her feelings which ultimately decreases their intimacy level).

Model of the etiology of anxiety, David Barlow, 1988
summaized by Clyde M. Feldman, 2008

A SUMMARY OF SIX TYPES OF ANXIETY PROBLEMS
(BASED ON DSM-IV)

SPECIFIC PHOBIA (6%)

<u>FEAR OF SPECIFIC NON-SOCIAL OBJECTS OR PLACES</u> (e.g., snakes, bats, rats, spiders, heights, flying, elevators, thunder, lightning, small spaces, needle, injections, the site of blood)

- Excessive or unreasonable fear AND anxiety reaction to specific objects or places that are perceived to be dangerous.

- Must cause significant distress or disruption to your normal routine.

GENERALIZED ANXIETY (5%)

<u>FEAR OF THE CONSEQUENCES OF NEGATIVE LIFE CIRCUMSTANCES AND FEAR THAT YOU WON'T BE ABLE TO COPE</u> (i.e., family, money, work, health)

- Chronic, excessive and unrealistic worrying and anxious feelings about two or more major life circumstances (e.g., about school, career, relationship, child's welfare) much of the time for at least 6 months duration - but NO panic attacks, phobias, or obsession.

- In addition to chronic worry, typically clients are keyed up and tense, irritable, fatigued, have difficulty concentrating, and difficulties with sleep.

- The generalized nature of the anxiety may relate to more core and global fears like failure, rejection, not being in control, not being good enough or perfect enough.

PANIC (5%)

<u>NO SPECIFIC FEARED STIMULUS BUT FEAR OF HAVING MORE UNEXPECTED PANIC ATTACKS IN AWKWARD SITUATIONS</u>

- Panic attacks - recurrent, unexpected, discrete moments of intense anxiety that come on suddenly and last 1 to 10 minutes. Symptoms include accelerated heart rate, chest pain, trembling, sweating, dizziness, light-headedness... also may feel like they are going to die, lose control, or go crazy.

- Ongoing worry and concern about having more attacks, usually at unpredictable times and in unexpected settings, and about the consequences of the attacks (will I be injured, what will people think). When attacks are "cued", the cue is often physical exertion, seeing a crowd, going into an elevator, etc.

- As fear of unexpected attacks increases, some people develop Agoraphobia (fear of "open spaces") or a fear of being in places where you might have a panic attack and escape or help is difficult and/or embarrassing (e.g., driving alone, public transportation, elevators, restaurants, crowds). They avoid or severely limit travel sometimes to the point of being housebound.

   ** Some people have Agoraphobia with no history of panic - (fear of having a heart attack, losing bladder control, etc.)

POST-TRAUMATIC STRESS (4%)
(Develops in 25% of those exposed to trauma - highest among assault victims)

<u>FEAR THAT A PAST TRAUMATIC EVENT WILL HAPPEN AGAIN AND/OR THE OUTCOME WILL OCCUR AGAIN</u> (natural (e.g., earthquake) or man-made disaster (e.g., fire), early abuse, witness and/or experience a violent crime, combat, and car accident)   [Duration must last 1+ months]

- Client experienced a traumatic event involving actual or threatened injury or death to oneself or others close to them AND experienced fear, horror, helplessness.

- Re-experiencing - emotionally and physically - of the traumatic event in the present: (1) in dreams, (2) flashbacks, (3) in response to triggers - objects, types of people, smells, places, time of day, that remind you of it.

- Symptoms of over-arousal including difficulty sleeping, difficulty concentrating, on guard (hypervigilant), easily startled, and easily irritable- brought to anger.

- Avoidance: (1) of people, places, and things that remind one of the event, (2) of conversations about the event, and (3) of thoughts and memories about the event. Sometimes the level of avoidance reaches a point of "disassociation" or shutting down of emotional and relational reactions, tuning out, "numbness".

SOCIAL ANXIETY (3%)

<u>FEAR OF SOCIAL SITUATIONS</u> (e.g., public speaking, dating, parties, social and family gatherings, using public restrooms, taking exams, eating in public)

- Excessive fear of AND anxiety reaction to social situations that may cause humiliation, embarrassment, disapproval, disgrace (you'll look stupid, incompetent, weak, panicky, etc.).

- Must cause significant distress or disruption to your normal routine.

OBSESSIVE-COMPULSIVE (2%)

<u>FEAR OF YOUR OWN THOUGHTS, IDEAS, IMAGES, OR IMPULSES</u>
(e.g., contamination, doing something violent to somebody, hitting someone with car, leaving door unlocked, leaving stove on)

- Obsessions - chronic thoughts, ideas, images, or impulses which are intrusive, unwarranted, and unwanted. People are aware that these are a function of their own mind.

- Compulsions - repetitive, ritualized behaviors that one feels driven to perform in order to prevent or neutralize the obsession and reduce their anxiety. (e.g., checking and cleaning rituals, counting, repeating certain words, arranging, etc.).

Summarized from DSM-IV by Clyde M. Feldman, 2005

EXAMPLES OF NEGATIVE AND POSITIVE THINKING FOR ANXIETY PROBLEMS

EXAMPLES OF ANXIOUS THINKING FOR SIX TYPES OF ANXIETY PROBLEMS

- ### SPECIFIC PHOBIA

    Airplanes seem to be crashing all the time these days.
    I don't know how elevators stay up.
    I'll suffocate in the elevator.
    I can't handle scary situations.
    I won't be able to handle the needle.
    The bridge could fall in while I'm on it.
    Dogs attack me because they see I'm afraid.
    I'll go crazy from the anxiety.
    No one else has this problem as bad as me.
    I'm so weak.
    I can't stand it.

- ### GENERALIZED ANXIETY

    I'm inadequate.
    I'm responsible for everything.
    I'm going to fail.
    Something terrible is going to happen.
    I'm never good enough.
    I can't handle anything.
    If people knew what I was really like, they'd reject me.
    Anxiety is a sign of weakness.
    I'm a failure.
    Things will never turn out well.
    I won't be able to fix it.
    I'll be left all alone.
    I'll be poor and living on the street.
    What if it's cancer, M.S., etc?
    What if the business never makes it?
    Nothing is working out.
    I don't have anything going for me.

I WON'T BE ABLE TO HANDLE IT IF IT DOESN'T WORK OUT.

- ## **PANIC**

    I'LL HAVE A PANIC ATTACK.
    I WON'T BE ABLE TO GET OUT OF HERE.
    MY HEART WILL START RACING.
    I'LL PASS OUT.
    I'LL HAVE AN ASTHMA ATTACK.
    I'M HAVING A HEART ATTACK.
    I'LL VOMIT.
    I WON'T BE ABLE TO BREATHE.
    I'M GOING TO DIE.
    I'LL EMBARRASS MYSELF.
    I WON'T BE ABLE TO GET HELP.
    I'LL LOSE CONTROL.
    PEOPLE WILL THINK I'M CRAZY.
    PEOPLE WILL SEE ME AND LAUGH.
    I MUST HAVE A BRAIN TUMOR.

- ## **POST-TRAUMATIC STRESS**

    WHAT HAPPENED IS MY FAULT.
    I SHOULD HAVE BEEN ABLE TO PREVENT IT.
    SOMETHING TERRIBLE COULD HAPPEN AT ANYTIME.
    I'M IN DANGER NOW.
    I CAN'T LET MY GUARD DOWN.
    I'M HELPLESS.
    YOU CAN'T TRUST ANYONE.
    NO ONE WILL BE THERE TO HELP ME IF I NEED IT.
    THERE'S NO POINT IN TRYING TO CONTROL ANYTHING.
    I HAVE TO BE ON ALERT AT ALL TIMES.
    IT'S BETTER TO AVOID POTENTIALLY DANGEROUS SITUATIONS.
    THE WORLD IS UNPREDICTABLE AND DANGEROUS.
    I'M POWERLESS TO PREVENT A CATASTROPHE.
    LIFE IS MEANINGLESS.
    I WON'T BE ABLE TO STAND ANOTHER LOSS.
    IF I GET TOO CLOSE TO SOMEONE, THEY'LL LEAVE OR DIE.
    WHY IS THE WORLD SO CRUEL?

- **SOCIAL ANXIETY**

    I'll look like an idiot.
    They'll see I don't have anything intelligent to say.
    I'll say something stupid.
    I'll freeze up.
    I'm boring.
    They can see how nervous I am.
    Everybody is looking at me.
    They're all better, smarter, funnier, etc. than me.
    They think I'm a fool.
    That was terrible.
    No one liked me.
    They're trying to exclude me and I probably deserve it.
    I blew it again.
    He doesn't like me...so there's probably something really wrong with me.
    If I disagree, they'll get mad at me.
    I can't show how weak I really am.
    I have to make a good impression.
    I have to get their approval.
    I'm odd.
    I don't have what it takes to be successful.
    I'm different from everyone else.
    Why would they want to listen to me?
    I won't have the answers.
    They won't believe me.
    They'll think "what's wrong with this guy"?

- **OBSESSIVE-COMPULSIVE**

    There are germs everywhere.
    I've been contaminated.
    I have to clean this right now or I'll go crazy.
    I could do or say something unacceptable without realizing it.
    If I don't wash my hands, I could spread germs to my whole family.
    What if I forgot to lock the door? I have to be sure. I'd better check.
    I'll feel better if I do X again.

BETTER SAFE THAN SORRY.
I'M A TERRIBLE PERSON FOR HAVING SUCH THOUGHTS.
THAT HORRIBLE THOUGHT'LL COME TRUE UNLESS I DO SOMETHING TO STOP IT RIGHT NOW.
IT HAS TO BE PERFECT.
THOUGHTS ARE POWERFUL AND CAN CAUSE BAD THINGS TO HAPPEN.
IF I CAN'T CONTROL MY THOUGHTS, I WON'T BE ABLE TO CONTROL MY ACTIONS.
I'M TO BLAME IF I DON'T TAKE ALL POSSIBLE PRECAUTIONS.
I'M THE ONLY ONE I CAN TRULY COUNT ON.

EXAMPLES OF POSITIVE COUNTER-THINKING TO USE IN ANXIOUS SITUATIONS

PREPARING EARLY BEFORE THINGS GET ANXIOUS

WORRYING WON'T MAKE IT GO BETTER.
WHAT EXACTLY DO I HAVE TO DO?
JUST THINK RATIONALLY. MY NEGATIVE THOUGHTS AREN'T VERY RATIONAL.
I CAN PLAN HOW TO DEAL WITH THIS BEFORE IT HAPPENS.
I KNOW I'LL GET BETTER WITH PRACTICE.
I'M GOING TO GET THROUGH THIS.
IT'S EASIER ONCE I GET STARTED AND JUMP IN.
TOMORROW I'LL BE THROUGH IT.
THIS IS GOING TO UPSET ME, BUT I CAN DEAL WITH IT.
WHAT IS IT THAT I HAVE TO DO?
I CAN WORK OUT A PLAN TO HANDLE THIS.
TRY NOT TO TAKE THIS TOO SERIOUSLY.
THIS COULD BE A NASTY SITUATION, BUT I HAVE TO BELIEVE IN MYSELF.

COPING WITH THE SITUATION WITHOUT BEING OVERWHELMED

I NEED TO TAKE IT ONE STEP AT A TIME AND GO SLOW.
REMEMBER TO BREATHE.
I CAN RIDE THIS THROUGH.
THIS IS JUST A FALSE ALARM... AN OVER-REACTION OF MY BODY.

I NEED TO LET THIS ANXIETY RISE AND FALL AND PASS.
THIS ISN'T DANGEROUS, IT'S JUST ANXIETY.
I CAN DO THIS… I'M DOING IT NOW.
THE TENSION I FEEL IS A SIGNAL TO RELAX AND THINK DIFFERENTLY.
I CAN GET HELP IF I NEED IT.
WHEN I DON'T SCARE MYSELF, I CAN HANDLE THIS MORE EASILY.
I DON'T HAVE TO LIKE THIS, I JUST HAVE TO GET THROUGH IT.
I'M SAFE RIGHT NOW.
IT'S JUST A MEMORY.
IF OTHER PEOPLE CAN DO THIS, SO CAN I.
THIS WILL BE OVER SOON, NOTHING LASTS FOREVER.
I'M ONLY THIS AFRAID BECAUSE I DECIDED TO BE.
I'LL GET USED TO THIS WITH PRACTICE.
I'VE SURVIVED THIS KIND OF THING BEFORE.
I CAN KEEP THIS WITHIN LIMITS THAT I CAN HANDLE.
FOCUS ON THE NEXT STEP.
FEAR IS NATURAL, IT GOES UP AND DOWN IN INTENSITY.
THERE ARE WORSE THINGS.
I NEED TO KEEP MY MIND OFF THIS AND ON WHAT I HAVE TO DO TO HANDLE IT.
I HAVE TO CONTINUE TO RELAX AND STAY CALM.
JUST GET A GRIP ON YOURSELF. YOU CAN HANDLE THIS.

GIVING MYSELF CREDIT AFTERWARDS

I'M GETTING BETTER WITH EACH TRY.
I CAN ACTUALLY CHANGE THIS.
I DID IT.
IT WASN'T AS BAD AS I IMAGINED.
MY THOUGHTS ABOUT IT ARE WORSE THAN THE THING ITSELF.
NEXT TIME, IT WON'T FEEL AS INTENSE.
I'M ABLE TO ACTUALLY RELAX WITH THE ANXIETY.
I SHOULD TELL ___ ABOUT THIS.

Modified and expanded from Robert Leahy & Stephen Holland, 2000

ANXIETY INVENTORY

1. Do you have spontaneous panic attacks that come out of the blue?
   Yes ___ No ___

2. Have you had at least four such attacks in the last month?   Yes ___ No ___

3. In your worst experience with panic, did you have four or more of the following symptoms?   Yes ___ No ___

   - [ ] shortness of breath or smothering sensation
   - [ ] dizziness or unsteady feeling
   - [ ] heart palpitations or rapid heartbeat
   - [ ] trembling or shaking
   - [ ] sweating
   - [ ] choking
   - [ ] nausea or abdominal distress
   - [ ] feelings of being detached or out of touch with your body
   - [ ] numbness or tingling sensations
   - [ ] flushes or chills
   - [ ] chest pain or discomfort
   - [ ] fear of dying
   - [ ] fear of going crazy or doing something out of control

4. Does fear of having panic attacks cause you to avoid going into certain situations?   Yes ___ No ___

5. Which of the following situations do you avoid because you are afraid of panicking?

   - [ ] going far away from home
   - [ ] shopping in a grocery store
   - [ ] standing in a grocery store line
   - [ ] going to department stores
   - [ ] going to shopping malls

- ☐ driving on freeways
- ☐ driving on surface streets far from home
- ☐ driving anywhere by yourself
- ☐ using public transportation (buses, trains, etc.)
- ☐ going over bridges (whether you're the driver or passenger)
- ☐ going through tunnels (as driver or passenger)
- ☐ flying in planes
- ☐ riding in elevators
- ☐ being in high places
- ☐ going to a dentist's or doctor's office
- ☐ sitting in a barber's or beautician's chair
- ☐ eating in restaurants
- ☐ going to work
- ☐ being too far from a safe person or safe place
- ☐ being alone
- ☐ going outside your house
- ☐ other _____

6. Do you avoid certain situations, not primarily because you are afraid of panicking, but because you're afraid of feeling social embarrassment or being negatively evaluated by other people?   Yes ___ No ___

7. Which of the following situations do you avoid because of a fear of social embarrassment or being negatively evaluated by other people?

    - ☐ sitting in any kind of group (at work, in school classrooms, social organizations, self-help groups, etc.)
    - ☐ giving a talk or presentation before a small group of people
    - ☐ giving a talk or presentation before a large group of people
    - ☐ parties and social functions
    - ☐ using public restrooms
    - ☐ eating in front of others
    - ☐ writing or signing your name in the presence of others
    - ☐ any situation where you might say something foolish
    - ☐ other _____

8. Do you fear and avoid any one (or more than one) of the following? But your avoidance is **NOT** due to a fear of having a panic attack or a fear of feeling social embarrassment? Yes ___ No ___

    ☐ insects or animals (spiders, bees, snakes, rats, bats, dogs, etc.)
    ☐ heights (high floors in buildings, tops of hills or mountains, bridges, etc.)
    ☐ elevators
    ☐ airplanes
    ☐ doctors or dentists
    ☐ thunder or lightning
    ☐ water
    ☐ blood
    ☐ illness such as heart attacks or cancer
    ☐ darkness
    ☐ other _____

9. Do you feel quite anxious a lot of the time but it is **NOT** because of fear of panic attacks or because of phobias, or social embarrassment?
    Yes ___ No ___

10. Have you been very worried for at least six months about two or more problems in your life such as finances, health, relationships, family, or school?
    Yes ___ No ___

11. Do you have at least six of the following symptoms because you're anxious and worried about the kinds of things in question 10? Yes ___ No ___

    ☐ trembling or feeling shaky
    ☐ muscle tension
    ☐ restlessness
    ☐ weariness or fatigue
    ☐ shortness of breath
    ☐ heart palpitations or racing heart
    ☐ sweating
    ☐ dry mouth
    ☐ abdominal distress or nausea
    ☐ lightheadedness or dizziness

☐ hot flashes or chills
☐ frequent urination
☐ lump in throat
☐ a feeling of being keyed up or on edge
☐ jumpiness or being easily startled
☐ difficulty concentrating or your mind goes blank
☐ trouble falling asleep or staying asleep
☐ irritability

12. Do any of the unpleasant thoughts listed below seem to enter your mind without you wanting them to. And although you know that they're irrational, you have a hard time keeping them from repeatedly coming into your mind?   Yes ___ No ___

   ☐ thoughts of being contaminated by dirt, germs, chemicals, or other substances
   ☐ thoughts of death or terrible things happening like fire, burglary, flooding, etc.
   ☐ thoughts of harm coming to a loved one because you weren't careful enough
   ☐ thoughts of you physically harming a loved one, poisoning someone, hitting a pedestrian with your car, pushing someone in front a moving vehicle, etc.
   ☐ thoughts of losing something valuable
   ☐ thoughts of a sexual or religious nature that normally are very unacceptable to you

13. Do you feel driven to do any of the behaviors listed below repeatedly or excessively? These behaviors often help relieve your anxieties about the thoughts in question 12.   Yes ___ No ___

   ☐ washing your hands, washing parts of your body, or grooming
   ☐ cleaning things
   ☐ checking lights, water faucets, the stove, door locks, or the emergency brake
   ☐ counting to yourself or repeating words or phrases to yourself
   ☐ touching objects or people in a certain way or a certain number of times
   ☐ arranging objects in a certain way or keeping things in a certain order
   ☐ doing certain actions a specific number of times or in a very specific way like when you go through a doorway or getting in/out of a chair, etc.

- [ ] avoiding certain colors, certain numbers, or certain names that you associate with unpleasant thoughts or events
- [ ] confessing that you said or did something incorrectly or wrong

14. Were you ever in a traumatic situation that made you feel intense fear, terror, or helpless - like being physically or sexually abused as a child, being the victim of domestic violence as an adult, being assaulted or raped, being present during a violent crime, being in a particularly bad car /plane/train accident, or being in a natural disaster?   Yes ___ No ___

15. If you said yes above, do you have any of the following symptoms which have lasted for at least one month or longer?

    - [ ] repetitive, distressing thoughts about the situation
    - [ ] nightmares related to the situation
    - [ ] flashbacks so intense that you feel or act as though the traumatic situation were occurring all over again
    - [ ] an attempt to avoid thoughts or feelings associated with the traumatic situation
    - [ ] an attempt to avoid activities or places associated with the traumatic situation (like a phobia about driving after you've been an car accident)
    - [ ] emotional numbness -or being out of touch with your feelings
    - [ ] feeling detached or distant from others
    - [ ] a loss of interest in activities that used to give you pleasure
    - [ ] anxiety symptoms, such as difficultly falling asleep or staying asleep, difficulty concentrating, being startled easily, or having a lot of irritability and outbursts of anger

Expanded from Edmund Bourne, 2000

ANXIETY INVENTORY SCORING

QUESTIONS 1, 2 3, 4 AND 5: PANIC DISORDER (with or w/o Agoraphobia)

If the answers to Q1 and Q2 were YES, it's likely you have PANIC.

If the answer to Q1 was Yes, but you had fewer than four attacks and/or fewer than four of the symptoms listed, than you likely DO NOT have full-blown panic disorder but rather LIMITED SYMPTOM ATTACKS.

If the answer to Q4 was YES, you may have Panic WITH AGORAPHOBIA. The number of situations checked in Q5 indicates the extent of the Agoraphobia and the degree to which it limits your activities.

QUESTIONS 6 AND 7: SOCIAL ANXIETY DISORDER

If the answer to Q6 was YES, it's likely you have SOCIAL ANXIETY. The number of situations checked in Q7 indicates the degree of the Social Anxiety problem.

QUESTION 8: SPECIFIC PHOBIA DISORDER

If one or more items in Q8 was checked, it's likely you have one or more SPECIFIC PHOBIAS.

QUESTIONS 9, 10, AND 11: GENERALIZED ANXIETY DISORDER

If the answers to Q9, Q10, and Q11 were YES, it's likely that you have GENERALIZED ANXIETY.

If the answer to Q9 was yes, but Q10 and/or Q11 were not, you likely have an anxiety condition that is not severe enough to be Generalized Anxiety.

QUESTIONS 12 AND 13: OBSESSIVE-COMPULSIVE DISORDER

If the answers to Q12 and Q13 were YES, it's likely that you have OBSESSIVE-COMPULSION.

If the answer to Q12 was yes, but Q13 was no, it's likely that you have Obsessive-Compulsion but have obsessions only.

QUESTIONS 14 AND 15: POST-TRAUMATIC STRESS DISORDER

If the answers to Q14 and Q15 were YES, it's likely that you have POST-TRAUMATIC STRESS.

IDENTIFYING CURRENT TRIGGERS

LIST EACH OF THE TRIGGERS THAT YOU HAVE AN OVERLY STRONG NEGATIVE EMOTIONAL REACTION TO (e.g., anxious, afraid, worried, humiliated, etc.). A TRIGGER CAN BE WHAT SOMEONE DOES OR SAYS, HOW SOMEONE ACTS, A TYPE OF SITUATION, A PLACE, CERTAIN OBJECTS, CERTAIN SOUNDS OR SMELLS, OR SOMETHING YOU SEE ON T.V. OR READ ABOUT. AFTER YOU LIST THE TRIGGERS, RATE EACH TRIGGER'S STRENGTH, INTENSITY, OR POWER FROM 1 (lowest) TO 10 (highest).

1. _____
   _____

2. _____
   _____

3. _____
   _____

4. _____
   _____

5. _____
   _____

6. _____
   _____

7. _____
   _____

8. _____

© Clyde M. Feldman, 2001

ANXIETY REACTION WORKSHEET

SITUATION: Describe the situation. It may be one where you were by yourself or with others.

_____

_____

_____

PHYSICAL AND EMOTIONAL REACTIONS: List as many as you felt and had.

_____

_____

_____

AUTOMATIC THOUGHTS: Write down the negative thoughts, beliefs, assumptions, expectations, and mental pictures that were going through your mind about yourself, other people, the situation, the future, etc. Also rate your belief in each of these from 1% (not really) to 100% (completely).

_____

_____

_____

_____

LEVEL OF ANXIETY: Rate the intensity from 1-10 (high) _____

OUTCOME: What was the actual outcome or result of the situation, which may have been very different than your worst fear or worry.

_____

© Clyde M. Feldman, 1994

TRAUMA REACTION WORKSHEET

SITUATION AND TRIGGERS: Describe the situation, especially the triggers like physical surroundings, sights, sounds, smells, things done or said, etc.

_____

_____

_____

_____

MEMORIES & SENSATIONS: List the negative, uncomfortable, or distressing memories or sensation that this situation triggered.

_____

_____

_____

AUTOMATIC THOUGHTS: Write down the negative thoughts, beliefs, assumptions, expectations, and mental pictures that were going through your mind about yourself, other people, the situation, the future, etc. Also rate your belief in each of these from 1% (not really) to 100% (completely).

_____

_____

_____

_____

LEVEL OF ANXIETY: Rate the intensity from 1-10 (high) _____

16 WAY TO RE-EVALUATE WHAT YOU SAY TO YOURSELF

1. What's the hard evidence for this being true? Have you really tested it out fully or did you just decide to <u>accept</u> it as true?

2. Does this hold true 100% of the time and in 100% of situations?

3. Do others agree with what you say to yourself and think it's healthy?

4. Has this always been true? Have you ever done anything in your life that was an exception to this or that contradicted this?

5. Is what you say to yourself flexible, have exceptions, and have grey areas or is it totally black and white, rigid, with no exceptions?

6. Who says? Compared to what? Compared to who? Based on what standard? Who decided that standard?

7. Is believing this good for you? Does it make you feel <u>better</u> about yourself, more in <u>control</u> of your life, better able to <u>cope</u> -or- does it make you feel worse, less in control, and less able to cope?

8. Does this keep you focused on the big picture, or does it keep you focused on one narrow aspect of things... like tunnel vision?

9. Do this make you <u>over</u>-emphasize and exaggerate the negative things and make you <u>under</u>-emphasize and minimize the positive things?

10. Is your rational, logical, and objective side telling you this -or- is it all based on intense feelings and emotions?

11. Is this something you <u>decided</u> to think and believe on your own, or did you get it from the past or from people like parents, etc.?

12. If you had a best friend in your situation, would you take the same attitude about them and their situation that you do about yours?

13. Image someone who's more like the way you wish you could be? Would they be saying the same things to themself as you do?

14. If you could magically get rid of this or take it less personally and less seriously, what would you be able to do, to feel, to believe, and to handle that you can't now?

15. What's the worst that could actually happen and how likely is that?

16. What would happen if you could stop saying this to yourself?
    Who's stopping you?

Modified and expanded from Robert Leahy & Stephen Holland, 2000

Clyde M. Feldman, Ph.D.

FOUR WAYS TO HELP CREATE POSITIVE SELF-TALK AND POSITIVE MENTAL PICTURES

YOUR POSITIVE PAST EXPERIENCE

Remember, think of, or find a time in the past, in a similar kind of situation when you were able to handle things more like you want to now. Remember that now and put yourself back into that situation. What were you able to say to yourself, believe, remind yourself, picture to yourself, feel emotionally, and do back then that would help you in the current situation?

FUTURE PROJECTION

Imagine that you could project yourself into the future (__ months / years from now), at a point in time when you have already figured out how to handle this kind of situation. What are you able to say to yourself, believe, remind yourself, picture to yourself, feel emotionally, and do in the future that would help you in the present?

A COACH OR MODEL

Think about someone - real or fictional, public or you know personally, living or passed away - who knows how to handle this kind of situation the way you wish you could. What would they coach you to say to yourself, believe, remind yourself, picture to yourself, feel emotionally, and do in the current situation? What would they be able to do say to themselves, picture, or do that you could try out for yourself?

A MAGIC WAND

Imagine you had a magic wand and you could use it on yourself to handle this kind of situation they way you wish you could. What would it give you the ability to say to yourself, believe, remind yourself, picture to yourself, feel emotionally, and do in this situation?

© Adapted from NLP and Solution-focused models by Clyde M. Feldman, 2010

The Therapist's Toolkit

POSITIVE COUNTER-STATEMENTS AND PICTURES WORKSHEET FOR REDUCING ANXIETY

WRITE DOWN YOUR NEGATIVE, ANXIOUS, FEARFUL, CATASTROPHIC THOUGHTS, BELIEFS, ASSUMPTIONS, EXPECTATIONS, AND MENTAL PICTURES WHEN ANXIOUS:

1a. _____

2a. _____

3a. _____

4a. _____

CREATE A POSITIVE COUNTER-STATEMENT, POSITIVE COPING STATEMENT, OR POSITIVE MENTAL PICTURE FOR EACH OF THE ABOVE:

1b. _____

2b. _____

3b. _____

4b. _____

© Clyde M. Feldman, 2001

SECTION 6:

STRESS TOOLS

EXTERNAL STRESS TEST

Please rate the items below in terms of how much stress you feel about each item. Use the rating scale::

0= NONE   1= A LITTLE   2= MODERATE   3= A LOT

WORK AND SCHOOL	0	1	2	3
Difficulties with a boss (or teacher)				
Difficulties with a co-workers (or other students)				
Too many tasks, responsibilities, deadlines, or pressures in work (school)				
Dull or boring tasks				
No rewards for work well done				
No opportunity for advancement				
Problems getting to where you need to go				
Problems finding a good job or keeping a job				
Not getting a fair salary for what you do				
No room for being creative				
Aren't listened to or can't give your input				
Too many changes in the organization				
Concerns about getting laid off or fired (or failing things in school)				
Having to re-train or go into a different line or work				
A work/school problem of mine not mentioned is _____				

SCORING FOR WORK AND SCHOOL

NO 2'S AND NO 3'S = **LOW STRESS**

NO 3'S AND UP TO THREE 2'S = **MODERATE STRESS**

ONE 3 <u>OR</u> HAVE FOUR OR MORE 2'S = **HIGH STRESS**

TWO OR MORE 3'S = **VERY HIGH STRESS**

PERSONAL AND SOCIAL LIFE	0	1	2	3
PROBLEMS GETTING ALONG WITH A CURRENT PARTNER (OR ROOMATE)				
PROBLEMS WITH AN EX-PARTNER OR EX-SPOUSE				
PROBLEMS WITH ONE OR MORE PARENTS				
PROBLEMS WITH BROTHERS, SISTERS, RELATIVES, OR IN-LAWS				
DIFFICULT BREAK-UP PROBLEMS OR SEPARATION PROBLEMS WITH A PARTNER				
PROBLEMS WITH HOUSEHOLD CHORES, TASKS, OR RESPONSIBILITIES				
MONEY PROBLEMS				
PROBLEMS RAISING OR MANAGING A CHILD				
PROBLEMS WITH ONE OR MORE FRIENDS				
NOT ENOUGH LEISURE TIME, VACATION TIME, OR TIME TO YOURSELF				
YOUR OWN OR SOMEBODY ELSE'S MEDICAL PROBLEMS				
YOUR OWN OR SOMEBODY ELSE'S ANXIETY OR DEPRESSION PROBLEMS				
YOUR OWN OR SOMEBODY ELSE'S PROBLEMS WITH ALCOHOL OR DRUGS				
PROBLEMS WITH LOW SELF-ESTEEM OR NOT FEELING GOOD ABOUT YOURSELF				
LEGAL PROBLEMS OR PROBLEMS WITH THE COURTS				
A PERSONAL/SOCIAL PROBLEM OF MINE NOT MENTIONED IS _____				

SCORING FOR PERSONAL AND SOCIAL LIFE

NO 2'S AND NO 3'S = **LOW STRESS**

NO 3'S AND UP TO THREE 2'S = **MODERATE STRESS**

ONE 3 OR HAVE FOUR OR MORE 2'S = **HIGH STRESS**

TWO OR MORE 3'S = **VERY HIGH STRESS**

© Clyde M. Feldman, 1999

THE INTERNAL STRESS TEST

There are actually two types of STRESS, **External** and **Internal**. External stressors are things like fighting a lot with your partner, in-laws who don't like you, not having enough money, raising a difficult child, or losing a job. Internal stress is more about you and the attitudes, rules, or ideas you may carry around about other people or yourself that can actually increase your stress level or make it worse than it actually is. Please put a number next to each stress statement using the rating scale below.

0= NEVER   1= RARELY   2= SOMETIMES   3= OFTEN   4= VERY OFTEN

1. Once I start something, I can't put it aside or delay it.... everything else has to wait.
2. In my head, I go back over things a lot that have upset me.
3. I don't make enough time to relax and let go of my tension.
4. I'm in a hurry and usually feel rushed.
5. I just can't let things "slide".
6. I take things personally a lot of the time.
7. I get very impatient with people.
8. I can't stand it when I have to wait in a line.
9. I usually try to get as many things done at once as I can.
10. I expect things to be done perfectly.
11. I'm hard driving and competitive.
12. I anticipate other people in conversation and often finish their sentences.
13. My mind is racing and I'm constantly thinking about things.
14. I spend a lot of time worrying about problems that I need to handle.
15. I find it difficult to say no to requests or demands.
16. I am very precise and detailed, and expect the same from other people.
17. I do everything myself and don't like to ask for help.
18. I hold my feelings inside and don't open up to other people easily.
19. I find it difficult to delegate tasks to other people.
20. I can't stand it when other people are late.
21. I can't stand it when other people leave things unfinished.
22. If I want something done right, I have to do it myself.
23. I need to get to the point in conversations without a lot of small talk.
24. I work a lot and have little time for play.
25. I feel as though I need to correct or fix other people's mistakes.
26. I get focused on very small details of things and miss the bigger picture.
27. I get very impatient if something doesn't happen the way I want it to.
28. I usually demand that I get attention or service immediately.
29. In traffic, I'm usually feeling frustrated or aggravated.
30. I focus on negative things in my life much more than positive things.

SCORING

Add up all 30 items = _____

If your score is 1 - 30, you probably have ***LOW INTERNAL STRESS***
If your score is 31 - 60, you probably have ***MODERATE INTERNAL STRESS***
If your score is 61 - 90, you probably have ***HIGH INTERNAL STRESS***
If your score is 91 - 120, you probably have ***VERY HIGH INTERNAL STRESS***

THE BEST ATTITUDE, RULE, OR IDEA I CAN HAVE ABOUT STRESS IS:

42 NEGATIVE CONSEQUENCES OF STRESS

- [ ] Headaches or pressure in head or temples
- [ ] Use "upper" type drugs more (cocaine, speed, meth, ecstasy, etc.)
- [ ] Have nightmares or bad dreams
- [ ] Criticize or blame others more
- [ ] Have a "negative" attitude more often
- [ ] Use alcohol more
- [ ] Over-eat more
- [ ] Lose your appetite or can't eat
- [ ] Smoke cigarettes more
- [ ] Have a hard time falling asleep or staying asleep
- [ ] Use pot or hash more
- [ ] Mind is often racing
- [ ] Diarrhea or constipation
- [ ] Nausea, cramps, or upset stomach
- [ ] Get sick more often than usual
- [ ] Fight and argue more with partner or family
- [ ] Use "downer" type drugs more (alcohol, GHB, heroin, etc.)
- [ ] More moody than usual
- [ ] Feel bad about yourself
- [ ] Lash out at people or things physically
- [ ] Forget things more than usual
- [ ] Can't get things done like before
- [ ] Sleep more than usual
- [ ] Make mistakes more often
- [ ] Act irritable or short-tempered more
- [ ] Feel depressed or discouraged
- [ ] Over-react to things
- [ ] Can't concentrate
- [ ] Feel very tired or exhausted
- [ ] Take on too many things at once
- [ ] Use "hallucinogen" type drugs more (acid, PCP, mescaline, mushrooms, etc.)
- [ ] Feel jumpy and nervous
- [ ] Don't feel comfortable alone
- [ ] Don't want to be around people
- [ ] Loss of sexual interest
- [ ] Act defensive more often
- [ ] Feel overwhelmed
- [ ] Desire to get away or escape from everything
- [ ] Take things the wrong way more often
- [ ] Grind teeth
- [ ] Say things you don't mean more often
- [ ] Tense, tight, or aching muscles

SCORING

TOTAL UP THE CONSEQUENCES YOU CHECKED= _____

IF YOUR SCORE IS 0-5, YOU PROBABLY HAVE **_LOW_ STRESS CONSEQUENCES.**

IF YOUR SCORE IS 6-10, YOU PROBABLY HAVE **_MEDIUM_ STRESS CONSEQUENCES.**

IF YOUR SCORE IS 11-20, YOU PROBABLY HAVE **_HIGH_ STRESS CONSEQUENCES.**

IF YOUR SCORE IS 21-42, YOU PROBABLY HAVE **_VERY HIGH_ STRESS CONSEQUENCES.**

© Clyde M. Feldman, 1994

SECTION 7:

SUBSTANCE ABUSE AND ADDICTION TOOLS

PERSONAL RISK PROFILE FOR ADDICTION

THERE ARE SEVERAL PERSONAL FACTORS BELOW THAT MAKE IT MORE LIKELY THAT YOU **COULD** DEVELOP A DRUG PROBLEM OR A DRUG ADDICTION. ALTHOUGH YOU MAY BE AT GREATER RISK, YOU HAVE THE POWER TO ULTIMATELY DETERMINE WHETHER YOUR FUTURE WILL BE HEALTHY OR UNHEALTHY.

1. **I HAVE A FAMILY MEMBER WHO CURRENTLY HAS, OR USED TO HAVE, A PROBLEM WITH ALCOHOL OR DRUGS.**

    A. NO

    B. YES...AND THE PERSON DIDN'T LIVE WITH ME GROWING UP AND ISN'T MY BIOLOGICAL PARENT OR BROTHER OR SISTER

    C. YES...AND THE PERSON DIDN'T LIVE WITH ME GROWING UP BUT IS MY BIOLOGICAL PARENT OR BROTHER OR SISTER

    D. YES...AND THE PERSON DID LIVE WITH ME GROWING UP BUT ISN'T MY BIOLOGICAL PARENT OR BROTHER OR SISTER

    E. YES....AND THE PERSON DID LIVE WITH ME GROWING UP AND IS MY BIOLOGICAL PARENT OR BROTHER OR SISTER

2. **ON A SCALE FROM 1 (LOWEST) TO 100 (HIGHEST), MY STRESS LEVEL OFTEN FEELS LIKE IT'S IN THE RANGE:**

    A. 1 - 50   B. 51-75   C. 76-100

3. **I CARRY AROUND ONE OR MORE UPSET FEELINGS INSIDE ME (LIKE SADNESS, ANGER, ANXIETY, SELF-DOUBTS, GUILT, LONELINESS, ETC) BECAUSE OF THINGS THAT HAVE HAPPENED TO ME OR MY CIRCUMSTANCES NOW.**

    A. HARDLY EVER

    B. SOMETIMES

    C. OFTEN

    D. MOST OF THE TIME

4. **I CAN USE THE SAME AMOUNT OR EVEN MORE ALCOHOL OR DRUGS THAN OTHER PEOPLE I KNOW AND NOT HAVE AS MANY BAD EFFECTS.**

    A. NEVER

    B. SOMETIMES

    C. OFTEN

5. **ONE OR MORE PEOPLE ACTED ABUSIVELY TO ME WHEN I WAS GROWING UP?**

    A. NO

    B. YES.... EMOTIONALLY ONLY

    C. YES.... PHYSICALLY OR SEXUALLY

6. **CHECK EACH OF THE PROBLEMS BELOW THAT YOU FEEL LIKE YOU CURRENTLY HAVE AND (1) YOU'RE NOT TAKING ANY MEDICATION FOR IT, OR (2) THE MEDICINE ISN'T WORKING VERY WELL.**

    ___ DEPRESSION   ___ ANXIETY/PANIC ATTACKS   ___ INSOMNIA

SCORING

Q1: A= 0 PTS, B= 0 PTS, C= 10 PTS, D= 15 PTS, E= 20 PTS

Q2: A= 0 PTS, B= 10 PTS, C= 15 PTS

Q3: A= 0 PTS, B= 10 PTS, C= 15 PTS, D= 20 PTS

Q4: A= 0 PTS, B= 10 PTS, C= 15 PTS

Q5: A= 0 PTS, B= 10 PTS, C= 15 PTS

Q6: EACH ONE THAT YOU CHECKED= 5 PTS

ADD UP THE POINTS YOU GOT FOR ALL SIX QUESTIONS

YOUR TOTAL RISK SCORE FROM 0 - 100% = _____

0-25% = LOW RISK, 26-50% = MODERATE RISK, 51-75% = HIGH RISK, 76-100% = VERY HIGH RISK

© CLYDE M. FELDMAN, 2001

ALCOHOL SELF-ASSESSMENT QUESTIONNAIRE

1. Have you ever felt you should cut down on, or tried to control (successfully or not), your drinking or drug use? **YES NO**

2. Have you ever felt bad or guilty about your drinking or drug use? **YES NO**

3. Do you ever take a morning eyeopener to steady your nerves or get rid of a hangover? Do you use drugs daily or weekly? Do you use prescription drugs more often than prescribed? Have you ever asked more than one doctor to prescribe a drug for you? **YES NO**

4. Are alcohol or drugs sometimes more important than other things in your life—your family, your job, your school, your values? Is drinking with your buddies more important than seeing your child in a school play? Is snorting coke more important than visiting your mom on her birthday? Is smoking pot all weekend more important than taking the make-up course you need to graduate? **YES NO**

5. Do you find yourself lying to your spouse, your kids, your friends, your employer, to cover up your drinking or drug use—though you really don't like lying? **YES NO**

6. Have you had problems connected with drinking or drug use during the past year (DUI's, lost work or school days, missed appointments, failed exams, financial problems, auto or other accidents with or without injury)? **YES NO**

7. Has your substance use caused trouble at home or work? Are those around you annoyed by or concerned about it? Are you annoyed by their concern? Do you become defensive? **YES NO**

8. Have you gone to work or driven a car while intoxicated, high, or in a drug-induced haze? **YES NO**

9. Have you been drunk or high more than four times in the past year"? Do you sometimes stay drunk for days at a time? **YES NO**

10. Do you need to resort to chemical assistance in order to do something (start the day, work, have sex, socialize, for example) or to change how you feel (sad, scared, anxious, or angry), to banish shyness or bolster confidence? **YES NO**

11. Have you ever switched from one kind of drink to another in the hope that this would keep you from getting drunk? Or from one drug to another to prove you're not addicted? **YES NO**

12. Do you notice you need more alcohol or more of your drug of choice in order to get a reaction? Can you handle more than before? More than most people? Or do you suddenly find you can't drink or drug as much?   **YES   NO**

13. Do you panic when you have to be somewhere where no booze or drugs will be available? Do you scrounge for extra drinks at parties because you feel you aren't getting enough? Do you keep going when everyone else has had enough?   **YES   NO**

14. Do you create situations where you can drink—like inviting friends over for a drink or arranging a meeting at a bar?   **YES   NO**

15. Do you panic when your bottle of pills gets low?   **YES   NO**

16. Do you sometimes carry booze or drugs around with you?   **YES   NO**

17. Do you tell yourself you can stop drinking or using drugs any time you want to, but find you keep getting drunk or high when you don't mean to?   **YES   NO**

18. Do you wake up the morning after with no memory of the night before? Have these blackouts— periods of which you have absolutely no memory—become more frequent?   **YES   NO**

19. Do the people you spend most of your time with drink too much or take drugs? Do you try to avoid other friends and family when you're drinking?   **YES   NO**

20. Do you do things while under the influence that you wouldn't do otherwise? Do you find yourself regretting them later?   **YES   NO**

21. Have you ever thought that your life might be better if you didn't drink or take drugs, or that life as it is just isn't worth living?   **YES   NO**

22. Has a doctor found signs of alcohol damage and warned you to stop drinking?   **YES   NO**

If you find the answer is "yes" to even two or three of these questions, you should seriously consider the possibility that your alcohol or drug use is a problem. If there are more than a few "yes" answers, you should seek help.

ALCOHOL AND DRUG INFORMATION

There are four major categories of substances that can lead you through a possible cycle of abuse, psychological dependence, or physical dependence and addiction. They all tend to tap into the pleasure centers of your brain. But they affect your body in very different ways and ultimately have negative effects on you physically and psychologically.

THE POTENTIAL CYCLE AND THE RISK FACTORS

USE ---> ABUSE ---> PSYCHOLOGICAL DEPENDENCE ---> PHYSICAL DEPENDENCE/ADDICTION

FAMILY HISTORY OF ABUSE OR DEPENDENCE	STRESS	EMOTIONAL "PAIN" (ANGRY, DEPRESSED, ANXIOUS, GUILTY, ETC.)	CAN USE MORE THAN OTHERS W/O THE SAME NEG. EFFECTS

DEPRESSANTS

HARD LIQUOR　　　　*MIXED DRINKS*　　　　*BEER & WINE*

OPIOIDS (PAIN KILLERS)　　*BENZOS* (VALIUM, XANAX)　　*DOWNERS*

GHB (LIQUID E, FANTASY)　*HEROIN* (JUNK, SMACK, HAMMER)　*METHADONE*

KETAMINE (K, SPECIAL K)　*ROHYPNOL* (ROPHIES, RUFFIES, R2)

INHALANTS (POPPERS, RUSH, WHIPPETS, LIQUID GOLD)

These drugs depress your central nervous system which makes you feel calm, relaxed, and less worried. The down-side is that as the amount increases in your body, they can cause drowsiness, dizziness, blurred vision, difficulty breathing, problems with your speech, attention, memory, judgment, and with sexual functioning. As you continue to use them they can cause nausea, insomnia, depression, aggressiveness, stomach ulcers, blackouts, and even heart failure. Longer-term use or high doses of HEROIN can cause clouded mental functioning, pneumonia, breathing problems, liver and kidney disease, heart attacks and strokes, blood clots, seizures, deterioration of while brain matter, and coma. Longer-term use or high doses of OPIOIDS can cause drowsiness, confusion, nausea, constipation, and slowed breathing. High amounts of GHB can cause amnesia, breathing problems, and impaired movement and speech, blackouts, and respiratory collapse. KETAMINE and ROHYPNOL are both tranquilizers and can have side effects including elevated blood pressure, tremors, hallucinations, confusion, and agitation. High amounts of many INHALANTS can causes nausea, blackouts, liver and kidney damage, heart attacks, and permanent brain damage. All of these drugs are potentially physically addictive, require more of the drug to achieve the same effects over time, and have withdrawal symptoms when you stop taking them or take less of them after heavy and repeated use. Withdrawal symptoms can include hand tremors, watering eyes, runny nose, hot and cold flashes, tingling sensations, heart palpitations, sweating, diarrhea and vomiting, headaches, stomach cramps, aches and pains, difficulty concentrating, insomnia, anxiety attacks, hallucinations, and seizures. While the risk of physical dependence on inhalants is relatively low, many users quickly become psychologically addicted.

☞ There is a growing opioid addiction epidemic in the U.S. Painkillers such as vicodin, oxycodone (percocet), morphine, fentanyl, and codeine are the most abused prescription drugs in the U.S. In 2019, almost 2 million people suffered from prescription opioid abuse problems and 50,000 people died from an opioid overdose.

☞ With all the publicity about how dangerous drugs are, it's easy to forget that ALCOHOL is still the number one "drug" problem in the U.S. About 15 million people (1 in 12 men; 1 in 25 women), have alcohol abuse problems. About 95,000 people die each year from alcohol-related causes. Among all auto accident fatalities, 28% are alcohol-related.

☞ Don't use alcohol in combination with one of these other drugs (often valium, xanax, or some type of downer). This is because each one has a sedative effect on your body so you are then multiplying this effect, which can lead to deep unconsciousness for several hours, coma, and even death.

☞ Inhalants are not illegal drugs, but are contained in common products like paint thinner, glue, nail polish, and things that come in aerosol cans - all of which are used to get high. They are abused most often by people between the ages of 7 and 17. Because they're common products, it's easy to forget that they are dangerous. Immediate death can result from a single inhalant use when the substance interferes with breathing or produces a highly irregular heart beat. Also, people have been known to suffocate in the bag they were using to concentrate the fumes. Long-term use can lead to liver and kidney damage, hearing loss, bone marrow damage, loss of coordination and limb spasms, brain problems and brain damage (from cut-off oxygen flow to the brain)

☞ Rohypnol is very much like valium, but **10 times** more potent. This has been labeled the "date rape" drug that has been given to females without their consent. Ketamine has become popular as a "club drug," because it is odorless and tasteless and can be added to beverages without being detected.

STIMULANTS

METH (SPEED, CRYSTAL METH, ICE, UPPERS)   *COCAINE (CRACK, BLOW, ROCKS)*

ECSTASY (E, X, ECCIES, MOLLY, DOVES)

These drugs stimulate your central nervous system which makes you feel high energy, alertness, tranquility, and a feeling of confidence. The down-side is that as the amount increases in your body, they can cause confusion, an inability to eat or sleep, nausea and vomiting, sweating, chills, agitation, tremors, boredom, anxiety, aggressiveness, rapid heart rate, seizures, blackouts, and coma. Longer-term use and high doses of METH or COCAINE can cause muscle spasms, confusion, irritability, hyperactivity, anxiety, aggressiveness, abdominal problems, malnutrition, insomnia, tremors, panic attacks, heart attacks, paranoid attacks, blackouts, and psychotic breaks. METH is also associated with memory loss, and severe dental problems where the users' teeth rot from the inside out. Longer-term use and high doses of ECSTASY can cause involuntary jaw clenching, lack of appetite, feeling "detached" from oneself, disorganized thoughts, restless legs, nausea, hot flashes or chills, headache, sweating, and muscle or joint stiffness. METH and COCAINE are physically addictive and you will experience withdrawal symptoms when you stop taking them or take less of them after heavy and repeated use. You can have vivid, unpleasant dreams, exhaustion, insomnia, eating binges, sweating, headaches, muscle pain, nausea and vomiting, physical pain, sense of confusion, depression, suicidal thoughts, anxiety, hallucinations, and seizures. They also tend to create a cycle where people have to keep using them to avoid the withdrawal symptoms. ECSTASY is not known to be physically addictive, but it is often used as a "club drug" in hot, crowded, dance settings and tends to prevent the brain from knowing that you are thirsty or very tired. This can lead to your body to overheat, and even lead to heat stroke, from not cooling down and not drinking enough water (drink only 20 oz. of water per hour).

☞ Up to 90% of these drugs can be "cut" or "filled" with one or more other drugs, to either increase the initial high (often use caffeine, aspirin, lidocaine, LSD, marijuana, heroin, speed) or add bulk to make them stretch farther (often use laundry detergent, boric acid, meat tenderizer, laxatives). Since they're made and sold illegally, it's anybody's guess as to what else may be in them.

MAJOR HALLUCINOGENS

PCP (ANGEL DUST, AMP)   ***MESCALINE (MUSHROOMS, CACTUS)***   ***LSD (ACID)***

These drugs affect your brain by altering your perceptions and mood, causing hallucinations, distorting what you see, hear, or taste, and altering your sense of time. The down-side is that they can also cause "bad trips" in which you may become anxious, disorganized, paranoid, panicked, enraged, afraid that you're going insane or are going to die. You can also lose touch with reality (try to fly). If you are worried or scared about taking it, or if something frightening suddenly happens, you can become severely anxious while you're using them. Other symptoms can include dizziness, nausea, numbness in extremities, blurred vision, sweating, uncontrolled eye movements, and tremors. Major Hallucinogens are not known to be physically addictive or have physical withdrawal symptoms. However, days or weeks after you stop taking them, you can keep having hallucinations (e.g., colors, images, halos).

MINOR HALLUCINOGENS

MARIJUANA (GRASS, POT, WEED)   ***HASHISH (HASH)***

These drugs affect your brain in a more minor way than the major hallucinogens do. Hashish is a potent form of cannabis, from 2x's to 6x's stronger. These drugs are not considered physically addictive, but can certainly be psychologically addictive. There is a growing movement in the U.S. to legalize recreational marijuana and to allow "medical marijuana" to be used for a range of medical benefits (epilepsy, pain, nausea). But it's important to realize that the potency of the active chemical THC in marijuana has increased dramatically over the years, from 1% in the 1970's, to 4% in 1998, to 15% in 2018. Some specialty plants can contain THC levels as high as 50%.

☞ While most people feel like there's not much of a down-side to using marijuana. However high doses and very frequent use is associated with several documented problems. High concentrations can cause paranoid feelings, panic attacks, and even LSD-type hallucinations. Frequent use can cause short-term and long-term memory problems. Long-term, frequent use can change your general personality, resulting in you being more unmotivated, more apathetic, taking the initiative less, and being less persistent at things.

TREATMENT RECOMMENDATIONS

1. Many people assume that they can solve a drug or alcohol problem without outside help. But prolonged exposure to drugs alters the brain in ways that result in powerful cravings and a compulsion to use. These brain changes make it extremely difficult to quit by sheer force of will. The need for some type of STRUCTURED PROGRAM, outpatient or residential inpatient, can be critical to getting stable (detox if necessary) and maintaining a healthy recovery. Outpatient options can include an individual counselor specializing in substance abuse individual or group counseling, an outpatient support group like A.A. or N.A., or an intensive outpatient program (I.O.P.) where very structured group and individual services are offered on an intensive, frequent schedule. Residential outpatient programs are the most comprehensive and usually provide a formal assessment, medical detox, individual and family counseling, and healthy lifestyle skills (meditation, yoga, healthy eating), and an aftercare component that helps transition back to your regular life. Residential stays are typically from 30 to 90 days.

2. MEDICATION-ASSISTED TREATMENT is now the preferred option for opioid addiction and more severe alcohol problems. Drug and alcohol problems are truly different than other mental health problems in that your body may be physically addicted to a substance, and the cravings and the withdrawal symptoms are not just psychological. Medications relieve the withdrawal symptoms and cravings that cause chemical imbalances in the body. Acamprosate, disulfiram, and naltrexone are used to treat alcohol abuse disorders. Buprenorphine, methadone, naltrexone, and naloxone are used to treat opioid disorders and prevent opioid overdoses.

Summarized by Clyde M. Feldman, 2021

TWENTY-ONE QUESTIONS TO ASSESS SEX ADDICTION

1. Has your sexual behavior either caused you to seek help or made you feel scared or different - somehow alienated from other people?

2. Do you keep secrets about your sexual or romantic activities from those important to you? Do you lead a double life?

3. Have your needs driven you to have sex in places or situations or with people you would not normally choose?

4. Do you find yourself looking for sexually arousing articles or scenes in newspapers, magazines, or other media?

5. Do you find that romantic or sexual fantasies interfere with your relationships with others or are controlling you?

6. Do you frequently want to get away from a sex partner after having sex? Do you frequently feel remorse, shame, or guilt after a sexual encounter?

7. Do you feel uncomfortable or upset when masturbating or touching your body? Do you avoid touching your body because of feelings of shame?

8. Does each new relationship continue to have the same destructive patterns which prompted you to leave the last relationship?

9. Have you ever tried to leave a specific person or a destructive relationship and found yourself returning?

10. Have you ever tried to limit or stop masturbating because of your discomfort with the frequency, your fantasies, the props you use or the places you masturbate?

11. Do you obsess about sex or romance even when it interferes with your daily responsibilities or causes emotional discomfort?

12. Do you avoid sexual relationships altogether, or for long periods of time, because they are just too difficult or not worth the trouble?

13. Does the time you spend reading pornographic magazines or watching films interfere with your daily activities and relationships with people?

14. Do you sometimes wonder if you are asexual or fear that you have no sexual feelings?

15. Do you lose your sense of identity or meaning in life without sex or a love relationship?

16. Is it taking more variety and frequency of sexual and romantic activities than previously to bring the same levels of excitement and relief?

17. Have you been arrested or are you in danger of being arrested because of your practices of voyeurism, exhibitionism, prostitution, sex with minors, indecent phone calls, etc.?

18. Does your pursuit of sex or romantic relationships interfere with your spiritual development?

19. Do your sexual activities include the risk, threat, or reality of disease, pregnancy, coercion, or violence?

20. Do you seek or use sexual or romantic highs to avoid unpleasant realities in your life? Do you find your basic needs and relationships are neglected following a sexual or romantic encounter?

21. Has your sexual or romantic behavior ever left you feeling hopeless or suicidal?

Sex Addicts Anonymous, 2007

SEXUAL ADDICTION

KEY COMPONENTS OF THE CYCLE

- **PREOCCUPATION**

    Excessive thinking about and fantasizing about getting that experience again, as well as dwelling on what, when, who, and where. Sex addicts believe sex is their greatest need.

- **COMPULSIVE SEXUAL BEHAVIOR**

    They can't control it and go to extreme lengths to get it. It is also marked by an absence of love and intimacy.

- **CONTINUATION DESPITE SOCIAL, OCCUPATIONAL, AND LEGAL CONSEQUENCES**

    It appears to provide a temporary relief and thrill. Most importantly, it functions to sooth and "self-medicate" an "empty hole" in themselves, feelings of shame, low self-worth, and issues of early abuse (87% were sexually abused).

- **SHAME, FRUSTRATION, GUILT, AND DESPAIR**

    Ultimately, they are left with intense negative emotional feelings because of a sense of loss of control - engaging in behaviors and not being able to stop. Substance abuse also commonly occurs as a result.

LEVELS OF SEXUAL ADDICTION

LEVEL ONE:
ACCEPTABLE AND TOLERABLE BY SOCIETY

Compulsive masturbation, compulsive pornography, a sexual fantasy life, anonymous sex (cruising, serial one-night stands)

LEVEL TWO:
VICTIMIZING BEHAVIORS THAT HAVE SANCTIONS

Exhibitionism (exposing oneself), voyeurism (peeping tom), obscene phone calls, masochism, sadism, and fetishism (using inanimate objects as sexual substitutes or symbols)

LEVEL THREE:
GRAVE VICTIM CONSEQUENCES AND SEVERE SANCTIONS

Child molestation, incest, rape, sexual violence

FOUR CORE BELIEFS OF THE SEX ADDICT

- I Am Basically Bad.

- No One Will Love Me As I Am.

- My Needs Will Not Be Met If I Depend On Others.

- Sex Is My Most Important Need.

Summary based on Patrick Carnes, 1992

SECTION 8:

TOOLS FOR OTHER RELATIONSHIP PROBLEMS

INTIMACY QUESTIONNAIRE

The two sets of 45 items below are about the quality of your relationship with someone. This might be a romantic partner, a spouse, a parent/child, a close friends, or even someone you work closely with. Think about that particular relationship when you answer the questions below. Use the scale:

0 = Not At All true / Doesn't fit
1 = Seldom True / Fits a Little
2 = Somewhat True / Fits Sometimes
3 = Often True / Fits Often
4 = Almost Always True / Fits Very Often

PART ONE: IN OUR RELATIONSHIP, I WOULD LIKE YOU TO:

1. Allow me more freedom. 0 1 2 3 4
2. Display more affection for me. 0 1 2 3 4
3. Have more respect for my judgment. 0 1 2 3 4
4. Feel more attached to me. 0 1 2 3 4
5. Treat me in a warmer and friendlier manner. 0 1 2 3 4
6. Allow me to feel more comfortable. 0 1 2 3 4
7. Go out with me more. 0 1 2 3 4
8. Feel more confident about my ability to think critically. 0 1 2 3 4
9. Allow me to make more decisions. 0 1 2 3 4
10. Display more love for me. 0 1 2 3 4
11. Accept and understand me for who I really am more. 0 1 2 3 4
12. Have more respect for my ability to think for myself. 0 1 2 3 4
13. Share more of your recreational time with me. 0 1 2 3 4
14. Tell me what to do less often. 0 1 2 3 4
15. Be more interested in me. 0 1 2 3 4
16. Be warmer and closer in your behavior toward me. 0 1 2 3 4
17. Act like I am a higher priority in your life. 0 1 2 3 4
18. Have more confidence in my ability to learn things. 0 1 2 3 4
19. Spend more time with me. 0 1 2 3 4

20.	Give me more freedom to choose my own friends.	0	1	2	3	4
21.	Be more interested in the things I am interested in.	0	1	2	3	4
22.	Spend more time alone with me.	0	1	2	3	4
23.	Put fewer limits on what I can do.	0	1	2	3	4
24.	Give me more praise for my accomplishments.	0	1	2	3	4
25.	Be there for me more when I need help or have problems.	0	1	2	3	4
26.	Give me more attention.	0	1	2	3	4
27.	Feel more love for me.	0	1	2	3	4
28.	Be more interested in being at home with me.	0	1	2	3	4
29.	Have more confidence in my ability to take care of myself.	0	1	2	3	4
30.	Allow me to think more for myself.	0	1	2	3	4
31.	Feel closer to me as a person.	0	1	2	3	4
32.	Feel more strongly that I am a good and likable person.	0	1	2	3	4
33.	Have more respect for my ability to solve problems.	0	1	2	3	4
34.	Go on trips and vacations more with me.	0	1	2	3	4
35.	Criticize me less for my conduct and behavior.	0	1	2	3	4
36.	Feel more strongly that I am an important person.	0	1	2	3	4
37.	Feel more confident about my ability to succeed at difficult tasks.	0	1	2	3	4
38.	Spend more of your free time with me.	0	1	2	3	4
39.	Supervise my activities less.	0	1	2	3	4
40.	Feel more affection for me.	0	1	2	3	4
41.	Be more confident that I can be trusted with responsibilities.	0	1	2	3	4
42.	Spend more time showing me how to do things.	0	1	2	3	4
43.	Include me more in things with other people.	0	1	2	3	4
44.	Feel more warmth for me.	0	1	2	3	4
45.	Engage more in activities with me.	0	1	2	3	4

PART TWO: IN OUR RELATIONSHIP, YOU WOULD LIKE ME TO:

1.	Allow you more freedom.	0	1	2	3	4
2.	Display more affection for you.	0	1	2	3	4
3.	Have more respect for your judgment.	0	1	2	3	4
4.	Feel more attached to you.	0	1	2	3	4
5.	Treat you in a warmer and friendlier manner.	0	1	2	3	4
6.	Allow you to feel more comfortable.	0	1	2	3	4
7.	Go out with you more.	0	1	2	3	4
8.	Feel more confident about your ability to think critically.	0	1	2	3	4
9.	Allow you to make more decisions.	0	1	2	3	4
10.	Display more love for you.	0	1	2	3	4
11.	Accept and understand you for who you really are more.	0	1	2	3	4
12.	Have more respect for your ability to think for yourself.	0	1	2	3	4
13.	Share more of my recreational time with you.	0	1	2	3	4
14.	Tell you what to do less often.	0	1	2	3	4
15.	Be more interested in you.	0	1	2	3	4
16.	Be warmer and closer in my behavior toward you.	0	1	2	3	4
17.	Act like you are a higher priority in my life.	0	1	2	3	4
18.	Have more confidence in your ability to learn things.	0	1	2	3	4
19.	Spend more time with you.	0	1	2	3	4
20.	Give you more freedom to choose your own friends.	0	1	2	3	4
21.	Be more interested in the things you are interested in.	0	1	2	3	4
22.	Spend more time alone with you.	0	1	2	3	4
23.	Put fewer limits on what you can do.	0	1	2	3	4
24.	Give you more praise for your accomplishments.	0	1	2	3	4
25.	Be there for you more when you need help or have problems.	0	1	2	3	4
26.	Give you more attention.	0	1	2	3	4
27.	Feel more love for you.	0	1	2	3	4
28.	Be more interested in being at home with you.	0	1	2	3	4

29.	Have more confidence in your ability to take care of yourself.	0	1	2	3	4
30.	Allow you to think more for yourself.	0	1	2	3	4
31.	Feel closer to you as a person.	0	1	2	3	4
32.	Feel more strongly that you are a good and likable person.	0	1	2	3	4
33.	Have more respect for your ability to solve problems.	0	1	2	3	4
34.	Go on trips and vacations more with you.	0	1	2	3	4
35.	Criticize you less for your conduct and behavior.	0	1	2	3	4
36.	Feel more strongly that you are an important person.	0	1	2	3	4
37.	Feel more confident about your ability to succeed at difficult tasks.	0	1	2	3	4
38.	Spend more of my free time with you.	0	1	2	3	4
39.	Supervise your activities less.	0	1	2	3	4
40.	Feel more affection for you.	0	1	2	3	4
41.	Be more confident that you can be trusted with responsibilities.	0	1	2	3	4
42.	Spend more time showing you how to do things.	0	1	2	3	4
43.	Include you more in things with other people.	0	1	2	3	4
44.	Feel more warmth for you.	0	1	2	3	4
45.	Engage more in activities with you.	0	1	2	3	4

Clyde M. Feldman, Ph.D.

SCORING:

FIND YOUR SCORES FOR THE **FIRST** 45 ITEMS ("I want you to"). THEN ADD UP THE SCORES IN EACH COLUMN.

CONNECTION	AFFECTION	AUTONOMY AND CONTROL
6. ____	2. ____	1. ____
7. ____	4. ____	3. ____
11. ____	5. ____	8. ____
13. ____	10. ____	9. ____
15. ____	16. ____	12. ____
17. ____	24. ____	14. ____
19. ____	26. ____	18. ____
21. ____	27. ____	20. ____
22. ____	31. ____	23. ____
25. ____	32. ____	29. ____
28. ____	35. ____	30. ____
34. ____	36. ____	33. ____
38. ____	40. ____	37. ____
42. ____	44. ____	39. ____
43. ____	_____ TOTAL	41. ____
45. ____		_____ TOTAL
_____ TOTAL		

THEN FIND YOUR SCORES FOR THE **SECOND** 45 ITEMS ("You want me to").
THEN ADD UP THE SCORES IN EACH COLUMN.

CONNECTION	AFFECTION	AUTONOMY AND CONTROL
6. ____	2. ____	1. ____
7. ____	4. ____	3. ____
11. ____	5. ____	8. ____
13. ____	10. ____	9. ____
15. ____	16. ____	12. ____
17. ____	24. ____	14. ____
19. ____	26. ____	18. ____
21. ____	27. ____	20. ____
22. ____	31. ____	23. ____
25. ____	32. ____	29. ____
28. ____	35. ____	30. ____
34. ____	36. ____	33. ____
38. ____	40. ____	37. ____
42. ____	44. ____	39. ____
43. ____	_____ TOTAL	41. ____
45. ____		_____ TOTAL
_____ TOTAL		

CONNECTION

0-16 The relationship appears to have a strong sense of feeling connected, included in each others' activities and lives, spending time together, being important and a priority, and being able to share private thoughts and feelings.

17-32 The relationship appears to have some, or even many, times of feeling connected, included in each others' activities and lives, spending time together, being important and a priority, and being able to share private thoughts and feelings. But problems exist in this area and it is definitely less than ideal.

33-64 The relationship appears to be suffering from not feeling connected enough, not feeling included in each others' activities and lives enough, not spending enough positive time together, not feeling important or enough of a priority, and not being able to share private thoughts and feelings.

AFFECTION

0-14 The relationship appears to have a strong sense of feeling close, feeling loving, getting/giving attention and compliments, with good amounts of physical and emotional affection being shown.

15-28 The relationship appears to have some, or even many, times of feeling close, feeling loving, getting/giving attention and compliments, with physical and emotional affection being shown but problems exist in this area and it is definitely less than ideal.

29-56 The relationship appears to be suffering from not feeling close enough, not feeling loving enough, not getting/giving enough attention or compliments, and not sharing enough physical and emotional affection.

AUTONOMY AND CONTROL

0-15 The relationship appears to be one in which independence and freedom as a separate individual can be maintained, you do not feel overly controlled/controlling or dominated/dominating, and you/they are treated as being capable of thinking and acting for oneself.

16-30 The relationship appears to be one in which sometimes independence and freedom as a separate individual can be maintained, you don't feel overly controlled/controlling or dominated/dominating, and you/they are treated as being capable of thinking and acting for oneself, but problems exist in this area and it is definitely less than ideal.

31-60 The relationship appears to be suffering from not being able to maintain independence and freedom as a separate individual, being overly controlled/dominated or being too controlling / dominating, and you/they are not treated like you/they are capable of thinking and acting for oneself.

THREE TYPES OF INTIMACY PROBLEMS

FEAR OF INTIMACY

Some indicators of a fear of intimacy problem MAY include: (1) being aloof with an "I don't need anybody" attitude, (2) being a loner and/or preferring to do things alone, (3) having a lot of buddies or acquaintances but few really close friends, (4) being unwilling to live with someone or get married, (5) not being able to be sensitive to other people's needs or empathize deeply (e.g., not giving a gift on special occasion, not showing much emotion when another gets into a car accident), (6) connecting intellectually but staying emotionally tuned out, (7) limiting what you reveal about yourself, (8) making everything into a joke, (9) sexuality looks and feels mechanical, and (10) feeling like you don't belong or fit in anywhere.

FEARS ASSOCIATED WITH INTIMACY:

- **FEAR OF EXPOSURE** - fear others will see physical, emotional, or psychological qualities of you that they will think are bad, will reject you, or will shame you with (e.g., body parts, being unlikable, things you're not good at, bad traits like being materialistic, selfish, domineering, drinking too much).

- **FEAR OF LOSS OF CONTROL** - fear of not having control over: (1) where the relationship is going or how fast/slow it is going there, (2) what the other person does or will do like work schedule, affairs, doesn't wear seat belt, who they chose as friends, (3) your own intensity of feelings/impulses in response to the person like your desires, your frustrations, or your anger.

- **FEAR OF LOSS OF ONE'S AUTONOMY/ INDEPENDENCE** - fear of having to do things you don't want to do, sacrifice and give-up things, or compromise on things and on your preferences (e.g., sex, talking, time to own's self, spending money, decorating, socializing, vacations, children-related, etc.)

- **FEAR OF ATTACK** - fear of being criticized, ridiculed, made to feel guilty, or even abused. This directly affects one's self-esteem and life in general because we become interdependent on the other.

- **FEAR OF DISAPPOINTMENT AND BETRAYAL** - fear that your expectations about the other person will not be met and you will be disappointed and letdown as you will see negative qualities you didn't realize were there and/or were different than you thought. This may be likely because people put on their best face and because you may use your sexual attraction as your guide. Fear that other person will lie, trick you, take advantage of you (e.g, use info against you, let you do all the work) or betray you.

- **FEAR OF GUILT** - fear that when anything goes wrong, you may blame yourself no matter whose fault it is. It's about taking on all the responsibility for how things go in the relationship (e.g., the other is unhappy, you don't want as serious a relationship as the other).

- **FEAR OF REJECTION AND ABANDONMENT** - fear that other will withdraw, take away their attention and affection, not be there for me, not want to spend much time with me, affairs, and actual abandonment.

OVERLY HIGH NEED FOR INTIMACY

Some indicators of an overly high need for intimacy problem MAY include: (1) others view you as needy or dependent, (2) having strong and immediate attractions to others, (3) being overly romantic, (4) thinking about or wanting to be with someone all the time, (5) not feeling O.K. being alone, (6) being unable or unwilling to let go of people or relationships like when they move, when they are unavailable, etc., (7) having extreme and dramatic reactions to relationship breakups like severe depression, suicidal thoughts, etc., (8) always sacrificing your own personal needs for the other person's needs, (9) not feeling O.K. without the love and approval of others, and (10) feeling lonely most of the time and feelings like nobody really knows you.

UNREALISTIC AND IDEALIZED BELIEFS & DESIRES ASSOCIATED WITH AN OVERLY HIGH NEED FOR INTIMACY:

- **REAL LOVE CONQUERS ALL** - it takes care of all problems, it has no hurts and pains, it takes away desire for others, it completes you.

- **REAL LOVE IS RARE** - and if it ends, it will devastate you and may well never come again.

- **REAL LOVE MEANS TWO BECOME ONE** - and giving up your separate self.

- **DESIRE FOR UNCONDITIONAL LOVE** - know me perfectly so I don't have to tell you. Love me and accept me no matter what.

- **DESIRE TO BE TAKEN CARE OF AND PROTECTED** - nurture me physically, emotionally, psychologically to the level of dependency and passivity - regressive. Protect me from the "dangerous" world and even from myself (set limits on own impulses, self-destructive behaviors)

- **DESIRE TO BE ADORED AS MOST SPECIAL** - make me the most important thing in your life, make me feel ok about myself, make me feel secure.

INCOMPATIBILITIES IN INTIMACY NEEDS

This type of intimacy problem occurs between partners with relatively normal intimacy levels (not the two problems above) who have significant differences in what they need and want in terms of: TOGETHERNESS, SEPARATENESS, PRIVACY, AND INDEPENDENCE. Usually this problem manifests as an ongoing battle or power struggle between one partner who become the PURSUER and the other partner who becomes the DISTANCER.

PERSUER VS. DISTANCER DYNAMICS:

- The PURSUER wants lots of shared activities and greater togetherness when stressed or anxious *BUT* the DISTANCER wants high amounts of private time and physical privacy, especially when stressed or anxious (e.g., separate rooms, vacations without partner, focused on solo hobbies)

- The PURSUER places a high value on talking and expressing feelings *BUT* the DISTANCER doesn't want to talk about things that are on their mind or express deep feelings, especially about things that's are bothering them.

- The PURSUER is a help-seeker and feels closest when they can show their vulnerabilities *BUT* the DISTANCER doesn't prefer to show their neediness and vulnerability.

- The PURSUER emphasizes their common beliefs, interests, tastes, and goals (symmetry) *BUT* the DISTANCER emphasize their distinct and separate identity with opinions, beliefs, interests, tastes, and goals that are not the same as the partner (complementarity).

- The PURSUER gets most upset and anxious when they feel "emotionally disconnected" *BUT* the DISTANCER gets most upset and anxious when they feel "smothered".

- A "Vicious" cycle can occur where the more one person pursues, the more the other person distances because they feel pushed, smothered, emotionally overwhelmed or intense. This increases the DISTANCER'S anxiety so they retreat and get more withdrawn. But the more that person distances, the more the other person pursues because they feel rejected and disconnected. This increases the PERSUER'S anxiety so they pursue they partner more vigorously to be reassured.

Summary of intimacy fears and needs based on Geraldine Piorkowski, 1994
Summary of persuer-distancer dynamics based on Harriet Lerner, 2005

JEALOUSY QUESTIONNAIRE

Please circle a number below for each item about jealousy, using the scale:

1	2	3	4	5
Strongly Disagree	Disagree	Neutral/ Somewhat	Agree	Strongly Agree

1. I have experienced a jealous "flash" or rush of feelings at least once.   1 2 3 4 5
2. I get a visual or mental picture of my partner with another person.   1 2 3 4 5
3. I am a highly competitive person.   1 2 3 4 5
4. I believe in monogamy (one partner) for an extended period of time or for life.   1 2 3 4 5
5. I am threatened when an attractive member of the same sex (reverse for gay/lesbian relationships) pays a great deal of attention to my partner.   1 2 3 4 5
6. I want to run away and hide when I feel jealous.   1 2 3 4 5
7. I feel powerless when I am jealous.
8. I get angry at myself when I am jealous.   1 2 3 4 5
9. I feel depressed or want to withdraw when I am in a jealous situation.   1 2 3 4 5
10. I try to make my partner jealous when I feel jealous myself.   1 2 3 4 5
11. When jealous, I feel unworthy of being loved.   1 2 3 4 5
12. I don't have many good qualities.   1 2 3 4 5
13. I am not well liked by my friends and family.   1 2 3 4 5
14. I am not very attractive.   1 2 3 4 5
15. I like to know where my partner is all of the time.   1 2 3 4 5
16. My partner does not believe in monogamy (one partner) for extended periods of time.   1 2 3 4 5

17. I am sometimes insecure about myself.   1   2   3   4   5
18. I have secretly followed my partner or listened in on a telephone conversation.   1   2   3   4   5
19. I have looked through my partner's purse or wallet.   1   2   3   4   5
20. I have "bad-mouthed" someone who is better than I am.   1   2   3   4   5
21. I don't seem to be able to maintain a permanent relationship because I am jealous.   1   2   3   4   5
22. I have asked to hear private details about a previous lover or partner.   1   2   3   4   5
23. I have wanted to run away from a party or situation where my partner has flirted with someone else.   1   2   3   4   5
24. I get angry at my partner when I am jealous.   1   2   3   4   5
25. I am afraid to get too close to a partner because I feel jealous.   1   2   3   4   5
26. I cannot cope with my partner having opposite-sex friends (reverse for gay/lesbian relationships).   1   2   3   4   5
27. I imagine situations where my partner is unfaithful.   1   2   3   4   5
28. My partner is physically more attractive than I am.   1   2   3   4   5
29. I am jealous about my partner's previous partners.   1   2   3   4   5
30. I do not have a lot of what I need in my relationship.   1   2   3   4   5
31. I should have better control over my jealous feelings.   1   2   3   4   5
32. I don't like to tell anyone that I am jealous.   1   2   3   4   5
33. I feel that only insecure people are jealous.   1   2   3   4   5
34. People have told me I have a bad temper.   1   2   3   4   5
35. I believe my partner and I should have an exclusive relationship.   1   2   3   4   5
36. My partner is the only person I "open up to."   1   2   3   4   5
37. I do not feel safe with my partner.   1   2   3   4   5
38. Sometimes I lose control of myself in the relationship.   1   2   3   4   5
39. I feel lonely.   1   2   3   4   5
40. I get aggressive when I feel jealous.   1   2   3   4   5

41. I am a romantic person.		1 2 3 4 5
42. My relationship with my partner is the most important thing in my life.		1 2 3 4 5
43. I cry easily.		1 2 3 4 5
44. I like the "old fashioned" or traditional way things used to be between men and women.		1 2 3 4 5
45. I am easily upset emotionally.		1 2 3 4 5

SCORING:

ADD UP ALL 45 RATINGS _____

0-150 = YOUR SCORE FALLS WITHIN THE NON-PROBLEMATIC RANGE. THIS LEVEL OF JEALOUSY CAN BE CONTROLLED BY THE INDIVIDUAL AND IS TYPICALLY NOT HARMFUL TO SELF OR OTHERS.

151-195 = YOUR SCORE FALLS WITHIN THE "POTENTIALLY PROBLEMATIC" RANGE. THESE JEALOUSY BEHAVIORS CAN BE UNHEALTHY AND EMOTIONALLY HARMFUL TO SELF OR OTHERS. PEOPLE CAN BEGIN TO FEEL OUT OF CONTROL, UNREASONABLE, OVERWHELMED, OR OBSESSED BY THOUGHTS OR IMAGES OF THEIR PARTNER WITH ANOTHER PERSON. THE PERSON MAY WANT TO SEEK REVENGE OR MAY WITHDRAW FROM OTHERS, OR BOTH.

196-225 = YOUR SCORE FALLS WITHIN THE "VERY PROBLEMATIC" RANGE. THESE JEALOUSY BEHAVIORS ARE VERY UNHEALTHY AND EMOTIONALLY HARMFUL TO SELF OR OTHERS. YOUR JEALOUSY RESPONSES MAY BE UNPROVOKED AND IRRATIONAL OR, EVEN IF YOUR REACTION IS PROVOKED, IT MAY BE EXTREME IN NATURE.

JEALOUSY PROBLEMS

A PERCEIVED THREAT OF LOSING A VALUED RELATIONSHIP OR A VALUED RELATIONSHIP COMMODITY TO A RIVAL

- **THE PERCEIVED THREAT** is experienced emotionally as anger, betrayal, distrust, hurt, or depressed. But the core emotion is FEAR and ANXIETY.

- **A VALUED RELATIONSHIP COMMODITY** that could be lost might include love, time together, attention, exclusiveness, confidante, status symbol, sex, social connection, power and influence, self-confidence, confirmation from the other of what is likable and good about you.

    For Males: the valued commodities lost are often sexual "rights", someone to rely on for domestic things, and a status symbol.

    For Females: the valued commodities lost are often love, a social bond, and intimate companionship.

- **THE RIVAL** is usually a person like a peer, co-worker, ex-partner, acquaintance, or relative stranger. But it can sometimes be a thing such as law school, hobbies, etc.

FOUR DETERMINANTS OF JEALOUSY PROBLEMS

1. **A HIGH LEVEL OF INVOLVEMENT AND COMMITMENT**

   When your level of involvement and commitment is strong, you typically have a strong sense of exclusivity of the relationship.

2. **HIGH PERCEIVED DOUBTS ABOUT THE OTHERS' INVOLVEMENT AND COMMITMENT**

   When the other person's level of involvement and commitment is different than yours and you view it as not as strong, worries would increase about: (a) your partner's attractiveness to others, (b) who they work around, and (c) how to interpret things that they do that make you wonder.

3. **HIGH DEPENDENCE ON THE RELATIONSHIP AND WHAT IT GIVES YOU**

   When you have high dependence on the person or relationship, the idea of losing rewards is significant because you probably feel you can't get them easily from others or give them to yourself.

4. **HIGH FEELINGS OF INADEQUACY AND POOR SELF-ESTEEM**

   When your self-worth is low and you're more insecure in general, the impact on you will be greater if you imagine you could be losing a person or relationship. You're also more likely to think that other people will see you as not O.K.

MANIFESTATIONS OF JEALOUSY

BOTH MALES AND FEMALES:

- **ACT POSSESSIVE** - monopolize partner's time, bragging about how much they're in love, kissing in public, etc.

- **MONITOR PARTNER** - spying, verifying, look through things, etc.

- **TRY TO GET BACK AT** - flit with others, get even, tell rival that partner has problems, std's, tell others that rival has problems, etc.

- **TRY TO WIN THEM BACK** - be more attractive to partner, improve relationship, do something to make partner jealous, etc.

FEMALES much more than males:

- **FEEL EMOTIONALLY DEVASTATED** - fear/anxiety, anger, sadness, betrayed, etc.

- **USE WITHDRAWAL AND AVOIDANCE** - physical & emotional withdrawal from partner, avoid jealousy-provoking situations or people, separate or end relationship.

- **TRY TO MAKE PARTNER AND OTHER PEOPLE THINK THEY DON'T CARE.**

- **CONFIDE IN A CLOSE FRIEND ABOUT THEIR FEELINGS.**

MALES much more than females:

- **GET AGGRESSIVE/THREATENING** - confront, threaten, be physical with the rival, demand that partner restrict their activities & contacts.

HOW TO IMPROVE JEALOUSY PROBLEMS

☞ **EVALUATE YOUR FEARS AND EXPECTATIONS.**

> How real are they?
> How likely is that to be true?
> How much are you exaggerating in your head?

☞ **BUILD SELF-ESTEEM, SELF-WORTH, AND INDEPENDENCE & AUTONOMY.**

> Know what positive qualities you have.
> Believe you can give yourself things if you can't get them from a partner.
> I'll be ok even if....
> I need to be independent enough to ....

☞ **BUILD MORE TRUST IN THE RELATIONSHIP.**

> Where does your lack of trust come from?
> What do you need your partner to do to increase your trust in them?

☞ **NEGOTIATE TO GET MORE OF WHAT YOU WANT IN THE RELATIONSHIP.**

> How satisfied are you with the relationship?
> What are you missing?   What needs aren't getting met?

Summaried by Clyde M. Feldman, 2005

Clyde M. Feldman, Ph.D.

INDEX OF RELATIONSHIP SATISFACTION

Think of your relationship over the last three months, and use the following words and phrases to describe it. For example, if you think that your relationship has been very happy, put an X in the box right next to the word "happy". If you think it has been very sad, put an X in the box right next to "sad". If you think it has been somewhere in between, put an X where you think it belongs. Make sure you <u>PUT AN X IN ONE BOX ON EVERY LINE</u>.

Miserable	[_]	[_]	[_]	[_]	[_]	[_]	[_]	Enjoyable
Discouraging	[_]	[_]	[_]	[_]	[_]	[_]	[_]	Hopeful
Tied down	[_]	[_]	[_]	[_]	[_]	[_]	[_]	Free
Distant	[_]	[_]	[_]	[_]	[_]	[_]	[_]	Close
Boring	[_]	[_]	[_]	[_]	[_]	[_]	[_]	Interesting
Disappointing	[_]	[_]	[_]	[_]	[_]	[_]	[_]	Rewarding
Brings out the worst in me	[_]	[_]	[_]	[_]	[_]	[_]	[_]	Brings out the best in me
Lonely	[_]	[_]	[_]	[_]	[_]	[_]	[_]	Connected
Hard	[_]	[_]	[_]	[_]	[_]	[_]	[_]	Easy
Worthless	[_]	[_]	[_]	[_]	[_]	[_]	[_]	Worthwhile
Hostile	[_]	[_]	[_]	[_]	[_]	[_]	[_]	Affectionate
Sad	[_]	[_]	[_]	[_]	[_]	[_]	[_]	Happy
Suspicious	[_]	[_]	[_]	[_]	[_]	[_]	[_]	Trusting
Separate	[_]	[_]	[_]	[_]	[_]	[_]	[_]	Together
Tense	[_]	[_]	[_]	[_]	[_]	[_]	[_]	Relaxed

All things considered, how satisfied or dissatisfied have you been with your relationship over the last three months?

COMPLETELY DISSATISFIED [_] [_] [_] [_] [_] [_] [_] **COMPLETELY SATISFIED**

Modified and expanded from Huston & Vangelisti, 1991

ROMANTIC LOVE BELIEFS QUESTIONNAIRE

The statements below relate to your beliefs about romantic relationships IN GENERAL. Please circle a number from 1 to 7 for each item using the scale below.

1	2	3	4	5	6	7
Strongly DISagree						Strongly Agree

1. Common interests aren't very important if you're truly in love. 1 2 3 4 5 6 7

2. As long as you know you're in love, it doesn't matter if you make a commitment after only a few days or weeks. 1 2 3 4 5 6 7

3. If you truly love someone, you can have a successful relationship even if you don't like their family or their friends. 1 2 3 4 5 6 7

4. Usually there's only one person in the world who you could really love and really be happy with. 1 2 3 4 5 6 7

5. The more in love you are, the more you want to "loose" yourself in the relationship. 1 2 3 4 5 6 7

6. Real love comes but once in a lifetime. 1 2 3 4 5 6 7

7. The end of a relationship is usually cause for deep despair. 1 2 3 4 5 6 7

8. If romantic partners love each other enough, problems or personality differences will never break them up. 1 2 3 4 5 6 7

9. If you were separated from a romantic partner for even a short, time, you would feel extremely lonely. 1 2 3 4 5 6 7

10. When you're finally with the right person, you won't feel attracted to other people. 1 2 3 4 5 6 7

11. When it's really true love, there won't be problems with things staying interesting or exciting. 1 2 3 4 5 6 7

12. In the ideal relationship, I would feel complete and whole. 1 2 3 4 5 6 7

13. An ideal partner would be able to give me everything that I need emotionally and would fill in the empty spaces in my life.   1 2 3 4 5 6 7

14. If two people love each other hard enough and long enough, they can solve their worst problems.   1 2 3 4 5 6 7

15. A relationship without emotional drama and lots of highs and lows is pretty boring.   1 2 3 4 5 6 7

16. True love can conquer all.   1 2 3 4 5 6 7

17. An ideal partner can complete you in most every way.   1 2 3 4 5 6 7

18. When you experience powerful sexual chemistry with someone, it's probably love.   1 2 3 4 5 6 7

19. If you really love someone, sometimes you need to punish them.   1 2 3 4 5 6 7

20. If your one true love ends, you'll probably never really love again.   1 2 3 4 5 6 7

21. In true love, you give up your individual identity so that two can become one.   1 2 3 4 5 6 7

22. If a wonderful romantic partner left me for someone else, I would be lost and be in deep despair for years to come.   1 2 3 4 5 6 7

23. In an ideal relationship, you would be thinking about your romantic partner day and night.   1 2 3 4 5 6 7

24. When I'm in a romantic relationship, I crave my partner physically, and emotionally, and mentally.   1 2 3 4 5 6 7

25. When a romantic partner doesn't pay attention to me, I feel very emotionally upset and troubled.   1 2 3 4 5 6 7

26. A romantic partner shouldn't be happy until they know that the other person is also happy.   1 2 3 4 5 6 7

27. You can't help feeling jealous when a romantic partner pays attention to someone else.   1 2 3 4 5 6 7

28. Being jealous of a romantic partner shows that you really care about them.   1 2 3 4 5 6 7

29. Purposely making a romantic partner jealous is a good way to get them to show if they really care about you.   1 2 3 4 5 6 7

30. You can't have too much love or closeness in a romantic relationship.   1 2 3 4 5 6 7

SCORING:

ADD UP YOUR SCORES FOR THE 30 ITEMS ABOVE ____.

30-105 =   YOUR ROMANTIC/LOVE BELIEFS SEEM PRETTY HEALTHY AND BALANCED.

106-150 =   YOUR ROMANTIC/LOVE BELIEFS COULD LEAD TO SOME INTIMACY DIFFICULTIES FOR YOU OR FOR A PARTNER.

151-210 =   YOUR ROMANTIC/LOVE BELIEFS ARE CAUSE FOR CONCERN AND CAN LEAD TO A RANGE OF INTIMACY PROBLEMS FOR YOU AND FOR PARTNERS.

Modified from Hatfield & Sprecher, 1986

Clyde M. Feldman, Ph.D.

ADULT ATTACHMENT STYLE QUESTIONNAIRE

The following statements concern how you feel in romantic relationships in general, not just about a current relationship. Please indicate how much you agree or disagree with the statements below using the scale below.

1	2	3	4	5	6	7
Strongly **DISAGREE**			Neutral/ Mixed			Strongly **AGREE**

___ 1.* I'd rather not show romantic partners how I'm feeling deep down inside.

___ 2. I worry about being abandoned.

___ 3.* It makes me uncomfortable when romantic partners get too close.

___ 4. I worry a lot about romantic relationships.

___ 5.* When romantic partners get too close to me, I tend to pull away and distance myself.

___ 6. I worry that romantic partners won't care about me as much as I care about them.

___ 7.* I find myself doubting the real motives of romantic partners.

___ 8. I worry a lot about losing romantic partners.

___ 9.* I worry about losing my independence in romantic relationships.

___ 10. I often get concerned about there being too much "separateness" in a romantic relationship, but rarely about there being too much "togetherness".

___ 11.* I want to get close to romantic partners, but I tend to pull back or withdraw a lot.

___ 12. I often want to merge completely with romantic partners and this sometimes scares them off.

___ 13.* It makes me feel nervous when romantic partners get too close to me.

___ 14. I worry a lot about being alone.

___ 15.* I feel uncomfortable sharing my most private thoughts and feelings with a romantic partner.

___ 16. My desire to be very close sometimes scares people away.

___ 17.* I often feel that romantic partners want too much from me.

___ 18. I need a lot of reassurance that I am loved by a romantic partner.

___ 19.* I often get concerned about there being too much "togetherness" in a romantic relationship, but rarely about there being too much "separateness".

___ 20. Sometimes I feel that I force a partner to show their feelings or their commitment.

___ 21.* I don't like relying on romantic partners too much.

___ 22. I often worry that a partner will not want to stay in the relationship with me.

___ 23.* When romantic partners want to be close, nurturing or affectionate, I often feel smothered.

___ 24. I can get pretty upset when romantic partners don't give me enough affection and attention.

___ 25.* I find myself holding back in romantic relationships to see if partners turn out to be honest and dependable.

___ 26. I find that romantic partners don't want to get as close as I would like.

___ 27.* Romantic partners have told me that I can keep a "wall" up that doesn't let them completely in.

___ 28. When I'm not involved in a romantic relationship, I feel anxious and insecure.

___ 29.* In romantic relationship, I need a lot of space.

___ 30. I have felt very jealous and possessive with romantic partners in the past.

___ 31.* I don't like to ask romantic partners for a lot of advice or help.

___ 32. Romantic partners have told me that I can act pretty clingy and dependent.

___ 33.* I'm concerned that the closer a romantic partner gets, the more I have to compromise.

___ 34. When romantic partners have disapproved or criticized me, I get really down on myself.

___ 35.* I don't prefer to turn to a romantic partner for comfort and reassurance.

___ 36. I resent it when a partner spends time away from me.

___ 37.* It's not easy for me to be affectionate with a partner.

___ 38. Sometimes romantic partners change their feelings about me for no apparent reason.

___ 39.* I'm concerned that I'll have to give up too much in romantic relationships.

___ 40. When a partner is out of sight, I worry that they might become interested in someone else.

Clyde M. Feldman, Ph.D.

SCORING ADULT ATTACHMENT STYLES

1. ADD UP ALL THE <u>ODD</u> NUMBERED ITEMS (ones with *) = _____

    IF YOUR SCORE IS 88 - 114, YOU HAVE A **MODERATELY AVOIDANT** STYLE.

    IF YOUR SCORE IS 115 - 140, YOU HAVE A **STRONGLY AVOIDANT** STYLE.

2. ADD UP ALL THE <u>EVEN</u> NUMBERED ITEMS = _____

    IF YOUR SCORE IS 88 - 114, YOU HAVE A **MODERATELY ANXIOUS** STYLE.

    IF YOUR SCORE IS 115 - 140, YOU HAVE A **STRONGLY ANXIOUS** STYLE.

3. IF YOUR SCORE FOR THE <u>ODD</u> ITEMS IS UNDER 88 AND YOUR SCORE FOR THE <u>EVEN</u> ITEMS IS ALSO UNDER 88, THEN:

    YOU HAVE A **SECURE** STYLE.

Modified from Bartholomew & Horowitz, 1991

THE THREE ADULT ATTACHMENT STYLES

SECURELY ATTACHED (55% of people)

Secure-style individuals often have good self-esteem and self-confidence. They view others as trustworthy, dependable, well-intentioned, and good-hearted. They like being involved in close interpersonal relationships. They seek and usually find a balance between closeness and togetherness, and between separateness and autonomy. They share intimate disclosures, show upset feelings about relationships without either bottling up feelings or over-dramatically expressing them, and seek help from others. They believe that real, romantic love does exist and can last.

AVOIDANTLY ATTACHED (25% of people)

Avoidant-style individuals often have good self-esteem and self-confidence. However, they view others with caution because they are concerned that others are not trustworthy, dependable, or honest - and often doubt their motives. They are often uncomfortable in, or tend to avoid, very close interpersonal relationships. They seek out separateness and autonomy. They have fears associated with intimacy and limit others from getting too close. They prefer to emphasize their independence and their personal and work goals. They tend to withhold intimate disclosure, suppress their upset feelings about relationships, and don't like to seek help from others. They believe that real, romantic love doesn't exist or, if it does exit, it doesn't last.

ANXIOUSLY ATTACHED (20% of people)

Anxious-style individuals often have lower self-esteem and have a number of self-doubts. They view others with caution and see others as complex and difficult to understand. They are concerned that others will misunderstand them, and will be unwilling to commit to them like they would want them to. They like being involved in close interpersonal relationships and seek out very high amounts of closeness, togetherness, and intimacy. They fear rejection and abandonment and get worried, upset, and anxious a lot about their relationships. They de-emphasize their own needs and focus more on others' needs. They tend to act clingy or dependent, and often need the approval of the other. They may show a strong sexual attraction early in a relationship, become jealous, or even obsess about the other person. They believe that real love exits but they can't seem to find it.

Summarized by Clyde M. Feldman, 2010

SECTION 9:

TOOLS FOR OTHER INDIVIDUAL PROBLEMS

NEGATIVE SELF-BELIEFS QUESTIONNAIRE

Rate each of the beliefs and attitudes below on a 1 to 4 scale. Each of these beliefs and attitudes will affect how you end up feeling, acting, and getting along in life. The 1-4 scale means:

1= Never / Not At All   2= Sometimes / Somewhat Agree

3= Frequently / Strongly Agree   4= Very Often / Very Strongly Agree

___ 1. I feel like a victim of outside circumstances.
___ 2. I feel like I'm not much of anything unless somebody loves me.
___ 3. Criticism is very upsetting to me.
___ 4. Success is everything.
___ 5. I hate being wrong.
___ 6. I feel that I'm not good enough.
___ 7. I can't rely on others for help.
___ 8 I feel a sense of defeat like "Why bother!".
___ 9. I feel like I'm not able to make it unless somebody loves me.
___ 10. If someone disapproves of me, I feel really bad about myself.
___ 11. I have to be somebody outstanding.
___ 12. I feel really bad about myself when I fail or make mistakes.
___ 13. I feel like I don't deserve to be successful or happy.
___ 14. I have a hard time receiving things from others.
___ 15. My situation seems out of my control.
___ 16. I can't feel happy and fulfilled unless I've got somebody who loves me.
___ 17. I need other people's approval to feel happy and good about myself.
___ 18. I have to be the very best at what I do.
___ 19. People would look down on me if they knew about all the mistakes I've made.
___ 20. I feel ashamed of who I am and of my situation.
___ 21. If I let someone get too close, I'm afraid of being controlled.
___ 22. I'm just the way I am - I can't really change that.
___ 23. I have to have someone who loves me to feel happy and good about myself.
___ 24. I often get defensive when someone criticizes me.
___ 25. What I accomplish at work/school is extremely important.

___ 26. I feel like I should be the perfect .... employee or professional or student or partner or lover or friend or parent or son/daughter.
___ 27. I feel ....unattractive or inferior or unintelligent or guilty or ashamed.
___ 28. I can't tolerate things being out of my control.
___ 29. It would be extremely difficult or even impossible to solve the problems in my life.
___ 30. If someone rejected me, I would feel pretty devastated and feel like something was really wrong with me.
___ 31. My self-esteem depends a lot on what others think of me.
___ 32. Falling short at goals and accomplishments is not ok.
___ 33. I should be able to endure any hardship.
___ 34. I feel a lot of anger inside, although I may or may not show it everyday.
___ 35. I'm the only one who can solve my problems.
___ 36. I don't believe I will ever feel truly happy or good about myself.
___ 37. I can't stand being separated from others.
___ 38. What other people think of me is very important to me.
___ 39. I feel very upset because I have not been successful in life.
___ 40. I should be able to find the right solution to every problem.
___ 41. I blame myself for most problems in my relationships with other people.
___ 42. It's risky to trust people.
___ 43. I don't have much control over things that go wrong.
___ 44. If a person I love doesn't love me back, I feel like it's my fault.
___ 45. I should try to be pleasant and nice no matter how I really feel.
___ 46. I am envious and jealous of people who are at the top of their careers, have social status, wealth, or fame.
___ 47. I should be able to do things myself and not have to ask for help.
___ 48. If someone gets upset with me, I usually feel like it's my fault.
___ 49. I find it very difficult to trust others completely.
___ 50. There's little anyone could do to help me solve my problems.
___ 51. I have a hard time spending time alone.
___ 52. I get very self-critical if I'm not able to please everybody.
___ 53. People who achieve a great deal are more worthwhile than those who do not.
___ 54. I shouldn't be tired or fatigued.
___ 55. People won't like me if they see who I really am.

___ 56. I find it very difficult to allow myself to depend on others.
___ 57. My upset moods are caused by things that are beyond my control.
___ 58. I'd be afraid to face the world out there on my own without a person who loves me.
___ 59. I feel very bad if someone is annoyed with me.
___ 60. I feel inferior to people who are more intelligent and successful than I am.
___ 61. I hate making mistakes.
___ 62. I need to keep up a front or other people will see what I'm really like.
___ 63. If I let someone get really close to me, chances are I'll get really hurt.

HOW TO FIND YOUR SCORE

YOU GET SEVEN DIFFERENT SCORES FOR SEVEN DIFFERENT AREAS:

AREA 1: PERSONAL CONTROL & PERSONAL POWER

SUM UP THE SCORES FOR ITEMS:

__ __ __ __ __ __ __ __ __ = __
1   8   15 22 29 36 43 50 57

AREA 2: THE NEED FOR LOVE

SUM UP THE SCORES FOR ITEMS:

__ __ __ __ __ __ __ __ __ = __
2   9   16 23 30 37 44 51 58

AREA 3: THE NEED FOR APPROVAL FROM OTHERS

SUM UP THE SCORES FOR ITEMS:

___ ___ ___ ___ ___ ___ ___ ___ ___ = ___
3   10   17   24   31   38   45   52   59

AREA 4: SUCCESS AND ACHIEVEMENT

SUM UP THE SCORES FOR ITEMS:

___ ___ ___ ___ ___ ___ ___ ___ ___ = ___
4   11   18   25   32   39   46   53   60

AREA 5: PERFECTIONISM

SUM UP THE SCORES FOR ITEMS:

___ ___ ___ ___ ___ ___ ___ ___ ___ = ___
5   12   19   26   33   40   47   54   61

AREA 6: SELF-ESTEEM

SUM UP THE SCORES FOR ITEMS:

___ ___ ___ ___ ___ ___ ___ ___ ___ = ___
6   13   20   27   34   41   48   55   62

AREA 7: TRUST

SUM UP THE SCORES FOR ITEMS:

___ ___ ___ ___ ___ ___ ___ ___ ___ = ___
7   14   21   28   35   42   49   56   63

WHAT YOUR SCORES MEAN

IF YOUR SCORE IN ANY AREA IS 22 OR MORE:

PERSONAL CONTROL & PERSONAL POWER

IT'S LIKELY THAT YOU BELIEVE THAT YOU'RE POWERLESS, HAVE LITTLE OR NO CONTROL OVER OUTSIDE CIRCUMSTANCES, OR AREN'T ABLE TO DO MUCH THAT COULD HELP YOUR SITUATION. THIS ATTITUDE WILL MAKE YOU EVEN MORE POWERLESS AND CAN LEAD TO A LOSS OF PERSONAL CONTROL AND EVEN TO DEPRESSION. THINGS MAY NEVER CHANGE BECAUSE YOU WON'T EVER TRY HARD ENOUGH TO CHANGE ANYTHING.

THE NEED FOR LOVE

IT'S LIKELY THAT YOU BELIEVE THAT YOUR SELF-WORTH AND HAPPINESS DEPENDS ON SOMEONE ELSE. YOU FEEL THAT YOU NEED ANOTHER PERSON'S LOVE TO FEEL O.K. ABOUT YOURSELF AND TO COPE WITH YOUR LIFE. YOU MAY ALSO HAVE A HARD TIME DOING THINGS BY YOURSELF AND BEING ALONE. THIS CAN LEAD TO YOU BEING A DEPENDENT PERSON RATHER THAN AN INDEPENDENT PERSON. IT CAN ALSO LEAD TO YOU BEING VERY EMOTIONALLY INSECURE AND NEEDY AND SOMEONE WHO MAY FALL APART WHEN RELATIONSHIPS END.

THE NEED FOR APPROVAL FROM OTHERS

IT'S LIKELY THAT YOU BELIEVE THAT YOUR SELF-WORTH DEPENDS ON WHETHER OTHER PEOPLE APPROVE OF YOU, AND AGREE WITH WHAT YOU THINK AND WHAT YOU DO. YOU MIGHT END UP SPENDING A LOT OF TIME PLEASING OTHERS AND CONSTANTLY TRYING TO GET ACCEPTANCE FROM OTHERS. THIS CAN LEAD TO YOU NOT REALLY KNOWING WHO YOU ARE OR DOING THINGS THAT YOU REALLY DON'T WANT TO DO BUT YOU THINK YOU SHOULD.

SUCCESS AND ACHIEVEMENT

IT'S LIKELY THAT YOU BELIEVE THAT YOUR SELF-WORTH DEPENDS ON EXTERNAL ACHIEVEMENTS AND ACCOMPLISHMENTS LIKE SCHOOL/CAREER PERFORMANCE, SOCIAL STATUS, OR WEALTH. THIS CAN LEAD TO CONSTANTLY NEEDING MORE AND MORE (MONEY, FAME, ACCOMPLISHMENTS) TO BE HAPPY. ALSO, IF YOU EVER LOSE ANY OF THESE THINGS, YOUR SELF-WORTH MAY CRASH AND BURN, BECAUSE YOU CAN'T FEEL GOOD WITHOUT THEM.

PERFECTIONISM

IT'S LIKELY THAT YOU BELIEVE THAT YOU HAVE TO BE PERFECT IN SOME OR MANY AREAS OF YOUR LIFE. YOU MAKE EXCESSIVE DEMANDS ON YOURSELF AND PROBABLY HAVE HIGH STANDARDS THAT OTHER PEOPLE CAN'T MEET. THERE IS NO ROOM FOR MISTAKES. THIS CAN LEAD TO FEELING CONSTANT STRESS AND PRESSURE EVEN OVER SMALL THINGS. YOU ALSO MAY HAVE A LOT OF TROUBLE LIVING WITH MOST OTHER PEOPLE SINCE THEY ARE NOT AS PICKY AND DEMANDING AS YOU. EVENTUALLY, YOU WON'T FEEL A LOT OF HAPPINESS OR PRIDE IN THINGS THAT YOU ACCOMPLISH AND DO WELL - BECAUSE WITH SUCH HIGH STANDARDS - YOU'LL THINK THAT YOU STILL AREN'T DOING GOOD ENOUGH.

SELF-ESTEEM

IT'S LIKELY THAT YOU BELIEVE THAT YOU AREN'T WORTH MUCH AND AREN'T O.K. DEEP DOWN. YOU PROBABLY HAVE LOW SELF-ESTEEM AND ARE VERY SELF-CRITICAL. THIS CAN LEAD TO A WIDE RANGE OF PROBLEMS INCLUDING: BEING EXPLOITED BY OTHER PEOPLE, BEING UNASSERTIVE AND NOT STICKING UP FOR YOURSELF, NOT GETTING WHAT YOU REALLY DESERVE, BEING DOWN ON YOURSELF ALL THE TIME, NEVER ACCOMPLISHING YOUR DREAMS AND GOALS, "SETTLING" IN LOVE AND ROMANCE, AND BLAMING YOURSELF FOR THINGS THAT ARE NOT ENTIRELY YOUR FAULT.

TRUST

IT'S LIKELY THAT YOU BELIEVE THAT YOU CAN'T TRUST, RELY ON, OR RECEIVE HELP FROM OTHERS. THIS CAN LEAD TO KEEPING A DISTANCE FROM PEOPLE AND AVOIDING BEING REALLY EMOTIONALLY INTIMATE WITH PEOPLE BECAUSE YOU'RE AFRAID OF NOT BEING THE ONE IN CONTROL OR AFRAID OF GETTING REALLY HURT. YOU'LL PROBABLY BE VERY JEALOUS AND SUSPICIOUS OF ROMANTIC PARTNERS EVEN WHEN THEY REALLY LOVE YOU AND ARE FAITHFUL. THIS CAN EVENTUALLY LEAD TO BEING SOMEONE WHO NOBODY REALLY KNOWS, BEING A SOCIAL LONER, AND FEELING LIKE LIFE IS A BURDEN BECAUSE YOU END UP HANDLING ALL THE HARD THINGS BY YOURSELF.

Edmund Bourne, 1995

NEGATIVE REACTION WORKSHEET FOR SELF-BELIEFS

SITUATION: Describe the situation. It may be one where you were by yourself or with others.

_____

_____

NEGATIVE FEELINGS: List as many as you had (over-sensitive, hurt, worthless, rejected, a failure, unworthy) and rate the intensity from 1 (low) to 10 (high).

_____

_____

_____

AUTOMATIC THOUGHTS: Write down the negative thoughts, beliefs, assumptions, expectations, and mental pictures that were going through your mind related to either your personal power, your need for love, approval from others, success, your perfectionism, your self-worth, or your trust in others.

_____

_____

_____

_____

_____

OUTCOME: How did your automatic thoughts end up making you feel worse about yourself, others, or keep you from handling the situation in the best way.

_____

_____

16 WAYS TO RE-EVALUATE WHAT YOU SAY TO YOURSELF

1. What's the hard evidence for this being true? Have you really tested it out fully or did you just decide to accept it as true?

2. Does this hold true 100% of the time and in 100% of situations?

3. Do others agree with what you say to yourself and think it's healthy?

4. Has this always been true? Have you ever done anything in your life that was an exception to this or that contradicted this?

5. Is what you say to yourself flexible, does it have exceptions, and does it have grey areas or is it totally black and white, rigid, with no exceptions?

6. Who says? Compared to what? Compared to who? Based on what standard? Who decided that standard?

7. Is believing this good for you? Does it make you feel better about yourself, more in control of your life, better able to cope -or- does it make you feel worse, less in control, and less able to cope?

8. Does this keep you focused on the big picture, or does it keep you focused on one narrow aspect of things... like tunnel vision?

9. Do this make you over-emphasize and exaggerate the negative things and make you under-emphasize and minimize the positive things?

10. Is your rational, logical, and objective side telling you this -or- is it all based on intense feelings and emotions?

11. Is this something you decided to think and believe on your own, or did you get it from the past or from people like parents, etc.?

12. If you had a best friend in your situation, would you take the same attitude about them and their situation that you do about yours?

13. Image someone who's more like the way you <u>wish</u> you could be? Would <u>they</u> be saying the same things to themself as you do?

14. If you could magically get rid of this or take it less personally and less seriously, what would you be able to do, to feel, to believe, and to handle that you can't now?

15. What's the <u>worst</u> that could actually happen and how likely is that?

16. What would happen if you could stop saying this to yourself? Who's stopping you?

Modified and expanded from Robert Leahy & Stephen Holland, 2000

FOUR WAYS TO HELP CREATE POSITIVE SELF-TALK AND POSITIVE MENTAL PICTURES

YOUR POSITIVE PAST EXPERIENCE Remember, think of, or find a time in the past, in a similar kind of situation, when you were able to handle things more like you want to now. Remember that now and put yourself back into that situation. What were you able to say to yourself, believe, remind yourself, picture to yourself, feel emotionally, and do back then that would help you in the current situation?

FUTURE PROJECTION Imagine that you could project yourself into the future (__ months / years from now), at a point in time when you have already figured out how to handle this kind of situation. What are you able to say to yourself, believe, remind yourself, picture to yourself, feel emotionally, and do in the future that would help you in the present?

A COACH OR MODEL Think about someone - real or fictional, public or you know personally, living or passed away - who knows how to handle this kind of situation the way you wish you could. What would they coach you to say to yourself, believe, remind yourself, picture to yourself, feel emotionally, and do in the current situation? What would they be able to do say to themself, picture, or do that you could try out for yourself?

A MAGIC WAND Imagine you had a magic wand and you could use it on yourself to handle this kind of situation they way you wish you could. What would it give you the ability to say to yourself, believe, remind yourself, picture to yourself, feel emotionally, and do in this situation?

© Adapted from NLP and Solution-focused modes by Clyde M. Feldman, 2010

POSITIVE COUNTER-STATEMENTS AND PICTURES WORKSHEET FOR NEGATIVE SELF-BELIEFS

WRITE DOWN YOUR NEGATIVE THOUGHTS, BELIEFS, ASSUMPTIONS, EXPECTATIONS, AND MENTAL PICTURES RELATED TO YOUR SELF-BELIEFS:

1a. _____

2a. _____

3a. _____

4a. _____

CREATE A SPECIFIC POSITIVE COUNTER-STATEMENT, POSITIVE COPING STATEMENT, OR POSITIVE MENTAL PICTURE FOR EACH OF THE ABOVE:

1b. _____

2b. _____

3b. _____

4b. _____

SEVEN TYPES OF COGNITIVE DISTORTIONS

When things happen in our lives, they don't lead DIRECTLY to us feeling something or doing something in response. In fact, it's well documented that first we go through an internal mental process that we often aren't aware of. That internal mental process involves filtering some situation or circumstance through our built-in assumptions, interpretations, perceptions, expectations, beliefs, and attitudes. We apply these cognitive filters, often unconsciously, to the situation, the circumstance, to what other people say and do, and even to what we say and do. Cognitive filters themselves are necessary and normal, but they can become distorted. Many individual and relationship problems can result from cognitive distortions in the way we view, perceive, and interpret things. Seven types of cognitive distortions are explained below.

1. **ALL-OR-NOTHING THINKING** involves looking at situations and people through an internal filter that creates black and white categories with no middle-ground or in-between area. We don't recognize that people and situations are a complex mixture of elements and rarely fall totally into one category or the other. There are two common types of all-or-nothing thinking. OVER-GENERALIZATION: We take things that happen and categorize them into groups that are at the extreme ends of the continuum, ignoring the middle-ground. For example, "She *never* appreciates anything I do", "He *always* rejects me", *"All* men are alike, they only care about themselves", "She's *always* late", "She *never* wants to have sex with me", "He *hates* me now", "It was a *complete* waste of time", "There's *not one* person in the world who cares about me". LABELING: We categorize ourselves and other people by applying all-or-nothing labels, usually negative ones. For example, if we make a mistake, we may tell ourselves "I'm a *failure*", "I'm an *idiot*". If someone else does something we don't like, we may think "He's a *loser*", or "She's a total *bitch*".

2. **JUMPING TO CONCLUSIONS** involves looking at situations and people through an internal filter that assumes we know why things happen, why people act the way they do, and how things will turn out in the future. We usually do this without having sufficient evidence and without really checking it out. There are two ways that people jump to conclusions. MIND-READING: We *decide* that we know why something happened or why someone acted the way they did before we *actually* know. We often decide that it was on purpose and the intention behind it was negative. For example, "She did it on purpose", "She knows how much that bothers me and did it anyway", "He doesn't even love me anymore", "She's doing this to get back at me", "He's probably cheating on me, that's why he's acting so

nice", "This is her little way of making me admit I was wrong." <u>FORTUNE-TELLING</u>: We *decide* that we know what will happen in the future and how things will turn out before we *actually* know. We often predict negative things will happen because they've happened that way before or because we don't think anything will ever change. For example: "She'll always act like a victim", "He'll never change his attitude", "There's no use in trying because it's not going to work out", "I'm really going to blow this", "The situation will never get better","I'm sure I failed the test", "There's no chance I'll even get a second interview", "That noise definitely means a major car repair and I can't afford that", and "My dog will eventually end up diabetic and that means she'll go blind".

3. **MAGNIFYING THE NEGATIVES** involves looking at situations and people through an internal filter that over-focuses on the negatives and exaggerates their importance and their impact. There are two ways to magnify the negatives. <u>NEGATIVE FILTERING</u>: We search for and single out the negatives and focus exclusively on them, even in the face of many types of positives. For example, a person focuses on one awkward interaction with a stranger at a party, even though all their other interactions went really well. Or a person receives twenty-seven positive comments about the presentation they gave, and one mildly negative one. They obsess about the negative one for days, and allow it to "cancel out" all the other positive comments. <u>CATASTROPHIZING</u>: We exaggerate the importance and impact of the negatives and, as a consequence, end up blowing things way out of proportion. Rather than being just annoyed or upset about something, our filter interprets the situation as *terrible*, *awful*, and *horrible*. Sometimes we do this because we're taking things too personally. For example, "I can't believe he said that, it's the worse thing I've ever heard", "These car problems will put me in the hospital", "I'll never travel again after that hotel fiasco", "If he puts me down one more time, I'll lock him out of the house", "This class is the most horrible thing that's ever happened to me", "I'll never trust a man again because of this breakup", and "I'd rather move than deal with this home owners' association".

4. **DISCOUNTING THE POSITIVES** involves looking at situations and people through an internal filter that overlooks, minimizes, or completely rejects the positives and their importance. There are two ways we discount the positives. First, we can **overlook and filter out the positives** by putting all our energy and attention into over-focusing on the negatives (i.e., magnifying the negatives). We can even minimize past positive experiences we've had by choosing to think about the negative ones more often and more intensely. Second, we may recognize the positives, but then **minimize them by deciding they "don't count"**. When we do something positive, or someone else says or does something positive, we can

discount it in a few ways. We can tell ourselves that it wasn't *that* good, it wasn't good *enough*, it was just *luck*, *anyone* could have done as well, or the other person didn't really *mean* the positive thing they said about us. This can lead to feeling inadequate and unrewarded.

5. **ASSIGNING BLAME** involves looking at situations and people through an internal filter that assigns too much blame to other people or to much blame to ourselves. When we **over-blame other people**, we often don't look closely enough at *our own* part in the problem. For example, "My parents screwed everything up and that's why nothing ever turns out right for me", "I'm not a perfect partner, but this one is all on him", "I wouldn't have cheated and had to lie about it, if she had paid an ounce of attention to me", "I dropped out of the program because none of these teachers know how to teach", "My marriage is falling apart because my spouse is totally unreasonable". When we **over-blame ourselves**, we often don't look closely enough at *other people's* part in the problem or how much the circumstances are actually under our control. For example, "It doesn't matter what she does wrong, I'm her mother and I'm to blame for not raising her right", and "I'm not good enough or I would've gotten that job".

6. **"SHOULD" EXPECTATIONS** involves looking at situations and people through an internal filter that makes "how things *should be*" always more important than "how things *are*". This results in taking our wants and desires and turning them into "shoulds", "musts", "oughts-tos" and "have-tos". It's not just a preference or request anymore, it's now an expectation or even a demand. **Applied to other people and the world in general**, "shoulds" create rigid expectations, rules, and demands about the way other people and the world *should be*, rather than focusing on managing and improving things the way they *are*. This often leads to feeling frustrated, angry, or a sense of righteous indignation. Since people don't like to be told what to do or told what's right or wrong, it makes it less likely they'll want to do things the way we think they should. For example, "She should do things that right way", "He has no right to be so argumentative", "People shouldn't get into debt in the first place", "He shouldn't lie to stay out of trouble", "How come I never win the lottery, but people that don't need the money always do?", "Why does everybody else have a happy marriage, but it's not in the cards for me?", and "I'm supposed to have grandchildren, but my daughter doesn't even want to have children". **Applied to ourselves**, "shoulds" create rigid expectations, rules, and demands about the way we *should be*, rather than focusing on how to manage and improve ourselves the way we *are*. This often leads to feeling discouraged, deprived, and depressed. For example: "I shouldn't have made so many mistakes", "I should've figured it out earlier", "If I were successful, I should have ___

by now". It's common for people to try and motivate themselves with "shoulds" and "shouldn'ts". For example telling ourselves, "I shouldn't eat that doughnut". At best, this can create battling parts of ourselves and internal conflicts. At worst, when the "shoulds" are punishing and demanding enough, this can lead to feeling defeated or being rebellious and doing the very opposite of what we *should* have done.

7. **EMOTIONAL REASONING** involves looking at situations and people through an internal filter that relies solely on your feelings to guide your perception and interpretation of situations and people. Our normally balanced use of *both* intellectual reasoning and emotions to guide us, can then get out of balance. As a result, we assume that how we *feel* accurately represents how things actually *are*. Even though our feelings are valid, they aren't always accurate. This can be especially true for negative feelings. For example, feeling terrified about going on airplanes would lead you to believe it must be very dangerous to fly. *Feeling* guilty would lead you to believe you must be a bad person. *Feeling* inferior around smart people would lead you to believe you have inferior mental capabilities or won't ever be smart enough to succeed. *Feeling* criticized by someone would lead you to believe that the person was purposely trying to put you down. *Feeling* rejected would lead you to believe that the person decided to actually reject you and doesn't want to be around you anymore. *Feeling* hopeless would lead you to believe that the situation is, in fact, hopeless.

Modified and expanded from David Burns, 1980

ADULT A.D.D. SCREENING QUESTIONNAIRE

The items below refer to how you have behaved and felt DURING MOST OF YOUR ADULT LIFE. If you have usually been one way and recently have changed, your responses should reflect HOW YOU HAVE USUALLY BEEN. Circle one of the numbers that follows each item using the following scale.

0= Not at all   1= Just a little   2= Somewhat   3= Moderately   4= Quite a lot   5= Very Much

1. At home, work, or school, I find my mind wandering from tasks that are uninteresting or difficult.   0 1 2 3 4 5

2. I find it difficult to read written material unless it is very interesting or very easy.   0 1 2 3 4 5

3. Especially in groups, I find it hard to stay focused on what is being said in conversations.   0 1 2 3 4 5

4. I have a quick temper...a short fuse.   0 1 2 3 4 5

5. I am irritable, and get upset by minor annoyances.   0 1 2 3 4 5

6. I say things without thinking, and later regret having said them.   0 1 2 3 4 5

7. I make quick decisions without thinking enough about their possible bad results.   0 1 2 3 4 5

8. My relationships with people are made difficult by my tendency to talk first and think later.   0 1 2 3 4 5

9. My moods have highs and lows.   0 1 2 3 4 5

10. I have trouble planning in what order to do a series of tasks or activities.   0 1 2 3 4 5

11. I easily become upset.   0 1 2 3 4 5

12. I seem to be thin skinned and many things upset me.   0 1 2 3 4 5

13.	I almost always am on the go.	0	1	2	3	4	5
14.	I am more comfortable when moving than when sitting still.	0	1	2	3	4	5
15.	In conversations, I start to answer questions before the questions have been fully asked.	0	1	2	3	4	5
16.	I usually work on more than one project at a time, and fail to finish many of them.	0	1	2	3	4	5
17.	There is a lot of "static" or "chatter" in my head.	0	1	2	3	4	5
18.	Even when sitting quietly, I am usually moving my hands or feet.	0	1	2	3	4	5
19.	In group activities it is hard for me to wait my turn.	0	1	2	3	4	5
20.	My mind gets so cluttered that it is hard for it to function.	0	1	2	3	4	5
21.	My thoughts bounce around as if my mind is a pinball machine.	0	1	2	3	4	5
22.	My brain feels as if it is a television set with all the channels going at once.	0	1	2	3	4	5
23.	I am unable to stop daydreaming.	0	1	2	3	4	5
24.	I am distressed by the disorganized way my brain works.	0	1	2	3	4	5

SUM UP ALL ITEMS: ____

SCORES OVER 70 ARE ASSOCIATED WITH A HIGH PROBABILITY OF A.D.D.

Disclaimer:
This is a screening examination for Adult ADD. It is not a diagnostic test. The diagnosis of ADD can only be made on the basis of a detailed history and mental status examination. High scores on this examination may result from anxiety, depression or mania. These conditions must be ruled out before a diagnosis of Adult ADD can be made.

© Copyright 1990, 1991, 1992, 1993 Larry Jasper & Ivan Goldberg

ADULT A.D.D. SIGNS AND SYMPTOMS

ATTENTION-RELATED DYSREGULATION

- Difficulty getting organized.

- Chronic procrastination or trouble getting started.

- Many projects going simultaneously; Trouble with follow-through.

- A frequent search for high stimulation.

- An intolerance of boredom.

- Easy distractibility, trouble focusing attention, tendency to tune out or drift away in the middle of a page or a conversation, often coupled with an ability to hyperfocus at times.

- Trouble in going through established channels, following "proper" procedure.

- Impatient; Low tolerance of frustration.

- Impulsive verbally, as in a tendency to say what comes to mind without necessarily considering the timing or appropriateness of the remark.

- Impulsive in actions, as in making impulsive decisions, impulsive in spending money, changing plans, enacting new schemes or plans.

- A tendency to worry needlessly and/or endlessly; A tendency to scan the horizon looking for something to worry about, alternating with inattention to, or disregard for, actual dangers.

- A sense of insecurity.

- Physical or cognitive restlessness.

- A tendency toward addictive behavior.

- Inaccurate self-observation.

- Often creative, intuitive, highly intelligent.

EMOTIONAL DYSREGULATION

- Mood swings; Mood may change frequently.
- Emotionally over-reacts.
- Overly emotional.
- May become emotionally upset easily.
- Experiences emotions intensely.
- A tendency to get "stuck" in an emotional state or can't get out of an emotional state easily.
- A tendency to get blind-sided (unexpected, surprised) by their own emotions.
- Particularly sensitive to rejection and teasing.
- A sense of underachievement, of not meeting one's goals (regardless of how much one has-actually-accomplished).
- A sense of insecurity.
- Chronic problems with self-esteem.

HISTORY

- Family history of ADD or manic-depressive illness or depression or substance abuse or other disorders of impulse control or mood.
- Childhood history of ADD. (It may not have been formally diagnosed, but in reviewing the history, one sees that the signs and symptoms were there.)

© Summarized and described by Clyde M. Feldman, 2021

PERSONAL AND RELATIONSHIP GOAL SETTING

Many times negative situations, problems, issues, and frustrations come up in our life and we know we need to solve them or improve them. But a lot of the time, they temporarily get moved to the back burner. Then something happens and we're reminded that they didn't go away and they're not really solved. A lot of times, we have good problem-solving skills, but still can't solve our problems very well. Often, that's because we have not taken the time to be clear about what the problems are AND WHAT OUR GOALS ARE. IN OTHER WORDS, WHAT WE WANT OR NEED TO BE DIFFERENT IN THE FUTURE.

PERSONAL DIFFICULTIES AND PERSONAL GOALS

THINK ABOUT YOURSELF, WHAT YOU'RE LIKE, AND WHAT YOU DO AND DON'T LIKE ABOUT YOURSELF.

Some problems, difficulties, or issues *about me personally* that I need to work on are:

1. _____

2. _____

3. _____

4. _____

THINK ABOUT THE THINGS YOU LISTED ABOVE IN TERMS OF WHAT YOU WANT OR NEED TO BE DIFFERENT IN THE FUTURE.

Some **shorter-term** goals *for me* are: (the next 4 months)

1. _____

2. _____

3. _____

Some **longer-term** goals *for me* are: (the next year)

1. _____

2. _____

RELATIONSHIP DIFFICULTIES AND RELATIONSHIP GOALS

THINK ABOUT YOUR CURRENT RELATIONSHIP OR PAST RELATIONSHIPS.

Some problems, conflicts, difficulties, and issues *in my relationship*(s) that I need to work on are:

1. _____

2. _____

3. _____

4. _____

THINK ABOUT THE THINGS YOU LISTED ABOVE IN TERMS OF WHAT YOU WANT OR NEED TO BE DIFFERENT IN THE FUTURE.

Some **shorter-term** goals *for my relationship(s)* are: (the next 4 months)

1. _____

2. _____

3. _____

Some **longer-term** goals *for my relationship(s)* are: (the next year)

1. _____

2. _____

© Clyde M. Feldman, 1994

A SUMMARY OF SIX MAJOR PERSONALITY DISORDERS (DSM-IV)

AVOIDANT PERSONALITY DISORDER
(more males than female)

CHARACTERISTICS

Social withdrawal is the key behavior. They are able to experience warmth and closeness and **need** to be included, accepted, and loved. They are eager to please, but have deep **fears** that others are uninterested, critical, and demeaning of them, so they tend to hang back in social groups, and back off or avoid getting involved in relationships. They feel tense, inadequate, threatened, insecure, inferior, foolish, humiliated, and shamed in social situations and close relationships. They exaggerate and are hypersensitive to being criticized, talked about behind their back, or seen for the inadequate person they believe they really are. They feel like they are being put on public display in social and work environments. They often have few close relationships aside from immediate relatives. They may have a significant relationship with someone if they're sure they will be liked and are reassured many times that the other person will be uncritically affectionate. They feel depressed and angry at themselves for social ineptness and awkwardness. They often are very successful at work that doesn't involve much social interaction or social skills. They may avoid any position that involves supervising others, rarely date, tend not to get noticed because they are so shy and timid, unassertive, and fearful of "competing" socially. They are often left feeling lonely and bored. Their **dilemma** is how to get affection and inclusion from people that they're afraid to associate with.

CORE BELIEFS

If I withdraw, nothing can hurt me. If people got close to me and really knew me, they would reject me. I can't handle these situations and terrible feelings... I need to wipe them out/distract myself (drink, drugs, etc.). I'm no good...worthless... unlovable. I can't take any risks or try new things socially. It's best to stay clear of involvement.. it's too risky.

ORIGINS

- May be based upon early experience of separation anxiety, inconsistent / neglectful nurturing, rejection, embarrassment, and humiliation (teasing) that instilled the idea that they will not be accepted and liked, overprotectiveness and cautiousness (not letting child explore) that relayed the idea that they are not competent.

© Summarized and described by Clyde M. Feldman, 2006

DEPENDENT PERSONALITY DISORDER
(more females than males)

CHARACTERISTICS

Over-dependence on others is the key behavior. They **need** to rely on others for a wide range of decisions, advice, reassurance and support about life's tasks and choices. They don't lack motivation, but rather confidence in their judgment or abilities. They see others as being nurturing, stronger, more competent than themselves and prefer others to handle major responsibilities for them. They seek out and cultivate intimate relationships with people they consider to be strong. They are typically clingy, submissive, unassertive, passive, accommodate to others wishes, won't make demands on others, and are reluctant to disagree. They are particularly needy and want support, caretaking, and approval when they are stressed. They have a hard time tolerating being alone and often feel anxious and helpless when alone. They deeply **fear** being left to care for themselves worried that significant people won't be there for them or will stop caring for them. They may interpret even small behaviors to possibly mean this (husband being late from work, friend cancelling lunch cause they're sick). Unfortunately, others may lose respect for them or take advantage of them or try to control them and they will tolerate this in order to maintain the relationship. (infidelities, drinking problems, and even abusive behavior). If a relationship ends, they will urgently seek a new supportive one. They often report getting less support and help than they'd like, and feeling anxious and lonely. Their **dilemma** is how to completely rely on someone that you know won't always be here.

CORE BELIEFS

I am helpless. I'm all alone. I can only function if I have somebody competent by my side. I can't live without person x. If I'm abandoned, I could die. If I'm not loved and supported, I will be unhappy forever. Don't offend them. Stay close to them. Try to please them. Be subservient.

ORIGINS

- May be based upon separation anxieties, inconsistent or neglectful nurturing; Early experiences of rejection, embarrassment, and humiliation (teasing); Overprotectiveness and cautiousness (not letting child explore) that relayed the idea that they are not competent or they can't operate independently; People either took total care of the child or didn't permit the emotional process of self-soothing, so they continually seek comfort when things feel bad.

© Summarized and described by Clyde M. Feldman, 2006

HISTRIONIC PERSONALITY DISORDER
(more females than males - 66% female)

CHARACTERISTICS

Being emotionally reactive and dramatic is the key behavior. They have a strong **need** to be the center-of-attention, to impress others, to get social approval, and get sympathy. They see others as admirers, as receptive and "seducible". They attempt to form strong connections with other people and are involved in many little details of the other person's life. However, this is with the unspoken agreement that they will be center stage and others will play the audience. They may dress and talk dramatically, "faint" at the sight of blood, dominate an entire party with tales of their recent faith healing, get so overcome with sadness at a movie that they have to be taken home immediately, and may even threaten suicide if a date's interest cools. They may need their friend to come right over if they're having an emotional crisis, wonder why no one called them after a traumatic visit to the dentist. They are very emotional and excitable but in a shallow-shifting way, often over-react to situations and events. They get easily frustrated when things don't go their way, throwing temper-tantrums, crying, getting assaultive, or even acting suicidal to either get their way or punish the offender. They are overly concerned with physical appearance, talk about themselves a lot, are inappropriately flirtatious and sexually provocative. They want love, but they deeply **fear** being ignored and not being center stage. They have a very hard time being in the background and can get angry and jealous when they're not acknowledged. Although at first they seem warm, affectionate, eager to please, and interested in others, relationships soon feel strained because they're demanding, manipulative, selfish, vein, shallow, and insincere. Their **dilemma** is how to keep people seeing you as the important center-of-attention when you're really shallow and insincere.

CORE BELIEFS

I need other people to admire me to be happy. I am lovable, entertaining, and interesting. People don't have the right to deny me. If I can't entertain and captivate people, I'm nothing and they'll abandon me. People that don't respond to me are rotten. I can always trust my feelings and let my feelings guide me. I'll pour out my affection if another person is affectionate to me, and pour out my hurt and anger if another person hurts me.

ORIGINS

- May be based on early experiences where parents offered no sympathy or empathy unless something really dramatic happened to you so dramatic displays get attention.

- May be based on overly puritanical parental values so the child over-reacts or goes to an extreme.

- May be based on parents reinforcing the child for their good looks and entertainment value.

- May be based on the lack of early praise or difficulty attaining it so child learns attention seeking.

© Summarized and described by Clyde M. Feldman, 2006

NARCISSISTIC PERSONALITY DISORDER
(more males than females)

CHARACTERISTICS

Acting very self-important, self-centered, entitled, and arrogant is the key behavior. They **need** to be admired and given special treatment because they are unique, better than others, gifted, and "above the rules". They may brag of their talents and achievements, predict great successes for themselves, like winning a Pulitzer prize, or rising up to the CEO of a company. They exaggerate their accomplishments, and often fantasize about fame, ideal beauty, brilliance, and success. They believe they should only associate with people of high-status and power. Paradoxically, they deeply **fear** that their abilities, talents, and superior position won't really measure up to their ambitions. And so they often feel bored, shallow or empty, even when they are successful. They see the vast majority of others as inferior, envious of them, and admiring. They closely monitor how others are viewing them and expect favors, compliments, adulation, and sympathy. They tend to run relationships based on what they can get from others. If others criticize them, slight them, or don't appropriately complement/flatter them, they may react in one of two completely different ways: with rage and contempt -OR- with despair and depression. They have a particular lack of empathy for other people's problems, worries, or pains (how statements may might hurt others, that a friend picking him up to go to party had to go to emergency room and he is more concerned about being late to party than health of friend). Ultimately, they have few if any genuine friends, but rather a group of loyal admirers. Their **dilemma** is how to value people's compliments and admiration when you hold those same people in contempt for being so inferior.

CORE BELIEFS

Since I'm special, I deserve special privileges. People should acknowledge that I'm superior to them. If they don't, they should be punished. To maintain my superior status, other people have to be subservient. I should strive for glory, wealth, position, power, and prestige - and demonstrate it to others at all times.

ORIGINS

- May be based on lack of early attention or approval so child over-compensates; Child was over-indulged and given inflated view of himself and his talents and his capabilities; Interactions that created a strong sense of inferiority so acting grandiose as a way for compensating for this.

© Summarized and described by Clyde M. Feldman, 2006

BORDERLINE PERSONALITY DISORDER
(more females than males - 75% female)

CHARACTERISTICS

Intense ambivalence (mixed extreme positions) about others in the form of extreme attachment along with extreme mistrust of others is the key behavior. The strong **need** for intense attachment, involvement, and dependency is related to having an unstable or under-developed sense of their own identity /self-image and so they define themselves in relation to others and often feel empty and unloved. The mistrust is related to a deep **fear** and anxiety that others close to them will victimize and ultimately abandon them. Relationships are stormy and intense because their moods can shift rapidly from being loving, sensitive, and involved to being enraged over being slighted, neglected, rejected, or betrayed. They are chronically angry below the surface, almost as though they are angry at the world. They also get very depressed, lonely, and grief-stricken at other times. They are very impulsive and even self-destructive and engage in shoplifting, gambling, over-spending, promiscuity, reckless driving, drug abuse, and suicidal threats and self-mutilating behavior. They see other people in their lives as "wonderful" sometimes and then horrible at other times (cruel persecutor). They have a hard time being alone and tend to be emotionally devastated when close relationships come to an end. Their **dilemma** is how to stay intensely attached while frantically avoiding being abandoned and victimized.

ORIGINS

- May be an extension of depression or manic-depression.

- May be based on early physical/sexual abuse where child develops a sense of rage but still has a need/desire to be loved in intimate relationships (70% had a history of sexual abuse).

- May be based on significant disruptions to parenting that caused emotional/psychological pain perpetrated by people that you thought would protect and care for you creates a deep-seated distrust/mistrust of others in close relationships (chaotic, threats of abandonment, real separations, incarcerations, averse to contact, withdrawal of affection, hostile, substance abuse, major psychiatric disorders).

© Summarized and described by Clyde M. Feldman, 2006

ANTISOCIAL PERSONALITY DISORDER
(more males than females - 80% male)

CHARACTERISTICS

Consistent disregard for and violation of rules and rights of others is the key behavior. This may include being aggressive, assaultive, or abusive to friends, family, and strangers, as well as stealing, lying, manipulation (con-artist), vandalism, prostitution, drug dealing, and pimping. They typically don't act responsibly or have a sense of obligation in work, relationship, financial, or family matters (walk out on job, children, etc.) They are often higher than average IQ, and do things on impulse, for thrills, and for immediate gratification as much as for personal gain. They seem to lack empathy and rarely feel remorse or shame for the harmful behavior they have committed. They are often superficially likeable, sociable, and even charming. They see other people as vulnerable and as objects to be used or exploited. They see themselves as loners, autonomous, and strong. They **need** to get what they want and deserve or else others will deny them or take it from them (**fear**). (70% of criminals in jail)

CORE BELIEFS

If you can get away with it, do it. I need to look out for myself. I need to be the aggressor or I will be the victim. Get them before they get you. Other people are patsies and wimps. If you let yourself be exploited, then you deserve what you get. If I don't push other people around, I'll never get what I want and deserve. It's my turn now, I've been the victim long enough. Take it, you deserve it. Rules were created by the "haves" for the "have-nots", so they need to be broken.

ORIGINS

- May be based on early physical/sexual abuse where the child models aggression from parents and others - OR - where the child develops a view of world such that no one cares about me (emotional indifference on part of adult), so why should I care about others (desensitize to fear, internalize indifference to others' pain).

- May be based on significant disruptions to parenting that caused emotional/psychological pain perpetrated by people that they thought would protect and care for them, which creates a deep-seated distrust/mistrust of others in close relationships (chaotic, threats of abandonment, real separations, incarcerations, averse to contact, withdrawal of affection, hostile, substance abuse, major psychiatric disorders).

- May be based on a coercive interaction style between the parent and child where child is resistant, has angry outbursts, throws temper-tantrums, or has an overly dramatic reaction and parents give up or give in after it escalates.

- May be based on underdeveloped frontal lobes where fear is not experienced normally and negative consequences are not processed normally.

© Summarized and described by Clyde M. Feldman, 2006

Made in the USA
Monee, IL
26 January 2025